Synchronization

Systemic Management

with the Goldratt Theory

Matías Birrell

Title: Synchronization – Systemic Management with the Goldratt Theory

First edition in English © 2018
ISBN-13: 978-1985302068
ISBN-10: 1985302063
All rights reserved by the author.

Author:
Matías Birrell

Preface

The concept of systemic thinking is very simple. It consists of treating systems as a whole different from its parts.

It is difficult to find someone who denies the systemic essence of almost everything in nature. That an ecosystem is a system in equilibrium is learned at a very early age. And that an apparently innocuous action on one of its parts can break the equilibrium of the ecosystem, altering it completely, it is something that we have learned by force, and it is also something of general culture.

By nature we understand the physical world, but we can extend the concept to all reality, including human organizations. This concept of system is also applicable here, so systemic thinking should be the basis of any method of managing organizations.

The idea is far from new. Russell Ackoff, Peter Senge, Jay Forrester, among many others, have said for decades that the organizations are systems and must be managed as such.

Management is a human invention. Like many other inventions, its prototypes had not functioned perfectly well the first time. And when any invention was based on a limiting principle, its operation was acceptable for not knowing anything better, but with the discovery of a new principle, the jump was extraordinary. An example is the airplane, which began its history powered by propellers. This limited the flying height and speed. With jet engines both of these limitations were moved to new levels.

But if in addition one of its principles is wrong, the improvement of the invention based on the correct principle, is phenomenal.

I believe that a large proportion of the Academy and the companies ignore a fundamental principle of management: its systemic nature.

In my opinion, the simplicity of the systemic approach is to understand what makes an organization more productive, and management should achieve more of that. And that something is the synchronization between the parts of the system. The symptoms that show us where we lack synchronization are always caused by conflicts, so that methodically eliminating conflicts is what it must be called scientific management.

Frederick Taylor was an American engineer known by many as the father of scientific management. He wrote a book[1] based on his experiences of decades, where he describes his methods of measurement of time and motion to improve productivity. And he is known by these same methods. As many things have changed today, the methods of Taylor are applicable to very few activities, for which I have heard more than one referring contemptuously to the scientific management of Taylor.

However, if one reads his book, will find in the first paragraph the following:

The principal object of management should be to secure the maximum prosperity for the employer, coupled with the maximum prosperity for the employee.[2]

That is to say, to eliminate the apparent conflict between the interests of the employer and those of the employee. Taylor followed the principle of synchronization, but what was left of his teachings were just suitable methods to eliminate such conflict in certain circumstances, but no one remembers the objective. Let be this quote to vindicate the memory of one of the great exponents of management discipline.

How many others have been misunderstood? It's hard to say. This book aims to sort this base of systemic thinking for management, highlighting the extraordinary contributions of Dr. Goldratt, because his Theory of Constraints is the best body of knowledge to implement the systemic thinking.

---

[1] The Principles of Scientific Management, Frederick Winslow Taylor, 1919.
[2] Ibíd.

I hope to have conveyed this idea with enough energy so that many programs of management education would recognize two things: how little is taught to think systemically nowadays, and how simple it is using the Goldratt theory.

There is surplus of empirical evidence to support everything said in this book. Goldratt Consulting already has many examples of transformation to systemic management. There is one in particular that I think it is impressive in terms of the magnitude and for the candor of the company to make it public. I am referring to Mazda Corporation of Japan. The year 2013, one of its senior directors, Mr. Mitsuo Hitomi, presented the case at an annual conference of TOCICO[3]. In this presentation, among other things, he said that with Theory of Constraints they had been able to return to profits after four years with large losses. But that is not all; he said literally that they had been saved from bankruptcy.

The purpose of this book is disruptive; it is intended to be the basis of the management systems of the future. A future with greater prosperity for everyone.

Matías Birrell Rodríguez
Santiago de Chile,
December 26th, 2017

---

[3] TOCICO: Theory Of Constraints International Certification Organization, www.tocico.org.

Contents

FUNDAMENTAL PRINCIPLES 1

THE FUNDAMENTAL ERROR 5
    INTRODUCTION 5
    THE FUNDAMENTAL ERROR IN THE 20TH CENTURY 7
    THE FUNDAMENTAL SOLUTION: A CHANGE OF ERA 10
    THE CONTRIBUTION OF DR. ELIYAHU GOLDRATT 14

LEAN: ENEMY N° 2 OF PRODUCTIVITY 23
    TOYOTA PRODUCTION SYSTEM 23
    LEAN MANUFACTURING: A PROVOKED CONFUSION 27
    LEAN AND 6-SIGMA TECHNIQUES WELL UTILIZED 33

SYSTEMIC APPROACH IN OPERATIONS 35
    INTRODUCTION 35
    PRINCIPLES OF FLOW 36
    MANAGING A FLOW 39
        Uncertainty 39
        WIP Control 40
    MAKE TO ORDER 42
        Capacity balancing 44
        Capacity buffer 45
        Production programming according to TOC 46
        Production control system according to TOC 48
        Buffer adjustments 49
    MAKE TO AVAILABILITY 50
        Inventory buffer 50
        Start up 51
        Continuity the next day 51
        Production control 52
        Buffer adjustment 53
        A warning 53
    PROJECT MANAGEMENT 54
        Planning process 54
        Critical Chain and Feeding Chains 56
        Programming of multiple projects 57

       Bad multitasking 57
       Mechanisms to avoid bad multitasking 59
       Control of execution in projects 60
       Summary 61
  DISTRIBUTION 62
       Planning and control of the supply chain 64
       Effects of reducing batches in cost 64
       Summary 66
  SUPPORT FUNCTIONS 67
       The problem 68
       Programming and control 69
  SUMMARY 70

SYSTEMIC APPROACH INCLUDING THE MARKET 73

  BLUE OCEANS 73
  UNSATISFIED SIGNIFICANT NEEDS 77
       Generic method to find significant needs 78
       How is the cause attacked and an offer generated? 79
  IMMEDIATE APPLICATIONS OF SYSTEMIC THINKING 80
       Reliability in delivery 81
       Increased inventory turns 85
       Availability 89
       Availability insurance 92
       Pay-per-click 94
  COMPETITIVE ADVANTAGES BASED ON INNOVATIONS 98
       Sources of innovation 101
       Improve value proposition 101
       Design the business model 105
  SELLING DECISIVE COMPETITIVE EDGES 106
       The three conditions for a sale 106
       The sale process 107

SYSTEMIC STRATEGIES FOR COMPANIES 111

  STRATEGIES AND TACTICS 111
  CONDITIONS OF A GOOD STRATEGY 112
  THE FUNDAMENTAL ERROR: ORIGIN OF CHRONIC CONFLICTS 115
  INNOVATION IS THE ONLY SUSTAINABLE STRATEGY 117

PERVERSE INCENTIVES 121

ELIYAHU GOLDRATT 122
DANIEL PINK 124
SIMON SINEK 125
FREDY KOFMAN 125
SUMMARY 127

POPULAR MYTHS IN MANAGEMENT 131

OPERATIONS 132
　Myth 1: An idle resource is always a waste 132
　Myth 2: The earlier I start, the sooner I finish 133
　Myth 3: The unit cost measures the real cost 134
　Myth 4: Improving the layout improves productivity 136
　Myth 5: Reducing setup times always brings benefits 138
　Myth 6: The more detailed the control, the more control is achieved 138
MARKETING 140
　Myth 1: It is possible to build a sustainable advantage based on cost 140
　Myth 2: The external environment is constantly changing 141
　Myth 3: The more positive differences, the more competitive the offer 141
SALES 142
　Myth 1: The purpose of the sales process is to sell 142
　Myth 2: Persuasion is an art with which one is born ... 143
　Myth 3: Salesmen must be good negotiators 143
　Myth 4: Commissions correctly incentivize salesmen 143
　Myth 5: The greater the magnitude of the change, the greater the resistance 144
　Myth 6: It is logical that greater volume has greater discount 145
DISTRIBUTION 146
　Myth 1: Larger inventory is required to offer better availability 146
　Myth 2: The closer the inventory is to the consumer, the better 146

Myth 3: Replenishing small batches reduces logistics efficiency.. 147
- STRATEGY 148
  - Myth 1: It is necessary to know the internal strengths before setting the course.. 148
  - Myth 2: The competition is a zero-sum game............ 148
  - Myth 3: It is important to be aware of the opportunities to take advantage of them all................................ 148
  - Myth 4: There are many independent factors that determine a strategy.. 149
- FINANCE 149
  - Myth 1: Greater profitability implies greater risk 149
  - Myth 2: With a more detailed budget, total spending is reduced... 150

ELIMINATING CONTRADICTIONS 153

- THE ORIGIN OF UNDESIRABLE FACTS 154
- TYPES OF KNOWLEDGE 157
- BASIC DISTINCTION BETWEEN OBJECTIVES AND ACTIONS 159
  - Objectives: a necessary agreement to advance 160
  - Validation of premises 161
  - Designing actions 164
- SUMMARY 165

SUMMARY OF SYSTEMIC MANAGEMENT WITH THE GOLDRATT THEORY 167

ANNEX: DECISION-MAKING EXERCISE 171

Synchronization

Systemic Management

with the Goldratt Theory

Fundamental Principles

In management of organizations, specifically of companies, there is, in my opinion, quite a bit of confusion.

I will show in this book that management is conceptually much simpler than it seems.

I express here the fundamental principles, which are developed further in the coming chapters:

- The generated value by companies is directly proportional to the synchronization that is achieved between its elements and related parties, both internally and externally.
- To manage is to make decisions that increase the synchronization and, therefore, the generated value.

If increasing synchronization is what increases the value generated by companies, it is very important to know what diminishes synchronization. To answer this question, it suffices to look at reality. We know there is a lack of sync every time you see a negative fact: we go to a store and we do not find what we want, or we need something to keep on working and we don't get it, or there is non-compliance with delivery commitments, failures in the quality, or at too great a cost.

A principle to support the development of the thesis of this book is that a negative fact is always the product of a contradiction or conflict.

If we observe a fact considered negative, there are two alternatives: either the responsible is negligent, or that it is very difficult to remove it. Let us put aside the first, which is a severe judgment, and by the large amount of negative effects we see on a daily basis, I am not convinced that the negligence is so widespread; this is my opinion. On the contrary, I believe that the majority of people try, diligently, to do the best possible job. We have the second alternative left.

Why would it be so difficult to eliminate a negative fact? We are all able to think of actions to eliminate it. But if those actions generate other facts just as negative or worse, we are caught in the contradiction between doing or not such actions.

> **Therefore, contradictions diminish synchronization. So eliminating contradictions, raises the value of the companies.**

Contradictions can always be removed with greater knowledge[4]. If it were possible to systematize the process to detect the contradictions, and to develop knowledge to eliminate them, the task of making the right decisions would be much more simple.

> **My claim is that the theory of Dr. Eliyahu Goldratt achieved precisely this: to identify and eliminate contradictions in a methodical and systematic way.**

To start mastering this knowledge is required to overcome a cultural problem, which, in the words of Russell Ackoff, will lead to a change of era.

---

[4] This is a statement that I will not attempt to demonstrate. It is a profound belief that drives all the thesis of the book, and corresponds to one of the principles of the Goldratt Theory.

Let us start at the beginning. The next chapter presents which is the fundamental error in the business culture that has contaminated the management for more than a century.

4

The Fundamental Error

Introduction

The year 1997, I read for the first time The Goal, a business novel written by Dr. Eliyahu Goldratt.

My first reaction at the end of the book was of unbelief. I already had several years of industrial experience and I thought that the novel should be fiction, because it had shown to me several errors that my bosses and I had continuously committed. They weren't errors as a result of incompetence or lack of diligence. They were errors by following what we thought were the best practices! And my resistance only lasted a few minutes: everything I read in that book was logical and common sense.

So I quickly realized that they were errors, but not necessarily mistakes. The distinction here is that a mistake is a judgment about the action - is committed wanting to do something else-, whereas an error is a judgment to the result. And many times the result obtained cannot be compared with what it was possible to obtain, and cannot be judged as severely as stated here, so there is not a questioning to the actions.

Time passed, and since the year 2006 I am working in the

company founded by Dr. Goldratt. In these years I have learned why those errors are committed, which cost a lot of money: it is for trying to do the best job possible! This seems to be a contradiction, however, it is the most logical conclusion: people are always trying to do the best possible.

The results are always the product of decisions [5]. And decisions are always based on a set of assumptions. And the set of assumptions shared by an organization is what we might call the culture of that organization.

My experience is that decisions are, the vast majority of the time, correct in the sense of being consistent with the set of assumptions. If other decisions have a much better result, it is obvious that the result of the first decisions can be referred to as an error. But if the decisions are consistent with the assumptions, and their results are errors, then it is not the managers who make poor choices; it is the set of assumptions which is wrong.

It is obvious that this reasoning can be applied to any set of assumptions, including the one that I am going to propose as correct in this book. Related to this, it was how Karl Popper defined a scientific theory. You can only call science to a theory that can be refuted with examples. And that is how knowledge progresses.

In this book, I will show you the most frequent and common errors, how their origin is in assumptions as widely accepted as incorrect, and what its consequences and solutions are. That is to say, I will show that most of the companies are managed today on the basis of assumptions that lead to results far worse than those obtained by adopting the assumptions that I am going to propose here. And we will be waiting for others that exceed what is proposed here, but in the meantime, we improve the quality of life of humanity with what we already know.

As we progress, you will see clearly that the solutions come

---

[5] It is obvious that there are many variables that cannot be controlled. However, the statement remains strong, otherwise it would not make sense to make decisions or to have managers at all.

from changing the assumptions that serve as a basis for decisions. As already mentioned, this set of assumptions accepted by the organization is the basis of their culture. The solutions proposed are nothing but a proposal for a cultural change.

A cultural change, also called a paradigm shift, is something that can be traumatic, so it is always difficult. The first reaction may be of denial. I had it. That is why I thought necessary to write a book that speaks explicitly of these errors, to remove the hand brake to productivity and growth.

I end this introduction with an insight: The success can be one of the most difficult obstacles to overcome in the path of learning and improvement. The good news is that there is still much to learn and improve, and I do not want to allow the success to prevent it.

The Fundamental Error in the 20th Century

What characterizes the majority of the organizations is that they are systems. My favorite definition of system is this:

> **A system is an interdependent set of elements with a purpose.**

The purpose of any system is to generate something that seems valuable to their members (or owners). I'll call it value to that something valuable. The value is created by the system as a whole.

> **The value created is the product of the interactions, as an emergent property of the system, and it is not possible for any of its parts to generate by itself.**

This statement is a fundamental assumption that I will use for the argument that follows.

To enunciate the most fundamental error in organizations, and particularly in the companies, committed in the 19th century,

20th century and to this point of the 21st century, I will ask a very basic question: why a salary is paid to people[6]?

First we understand that a company pays something in exchange for a value delivered. Therefore, the first answer is that the salary is paid in exchange for something of value.

As we have just established, the value that the system creates is the product of the interactions. Therefore, the salary is not paid in exchange for the individual action of the person only, but in exchange of their action can be synchronized with the other parts of the system to produce the value. If this is the case, the phrase "I'll pay for work" is wrong. In fact the company pays for having people available to make their contribution when required, in the value chain that makes up the system; and not to be occupied, working.

Let us remember this to connect it to another concept, the constraint, which I discuss below.

Dr. Goldratt used a very simple metaphor to explain the concept of constraint. He said that a company is like a chain, where each link has to do its part to generate the resistance of the chain as a whole. What determines the resistance of the entire chain? The weakest link. And how many weakest links does a chain have? One. The rest of the links have more resistance than the weakest, so they do not use their full capacity all the time.

This concept of constraint is known by mathematicians for a long time. And in the 40-50s, when the operations research arose about to support the activities of the Second World War, the mathematical programming was added to this set of techniques to study complex systems. The linear and non-linear systems, with continuous and discrete variable. These mathematical techniques are looking for optimum of systems considering the constraints. The constraints that determine the optimal, that is to say, all their capacity was used, are called active constraints.

This means that in an instant, we will see that the system has

---

[6] This is an another way to formulate the Elliot Jacques's conundrum.

an active constraint and the rest of its elements do not need to be working at its maximum capacity all the time.

Remembering what we have already said, that people receive their salary to be available when it is needed, and what we now know that the vast majority of the people are not "active constraints", then we can deduce that the salary is paid to the majority of people to be without work to do in many moments of time.

What is perceived at all levels in companies is the opposite: the prevailing ethic at work is that people must be busy. But we already know that the system works better with many resources idle from time to time.

We all love to find idle resources when we need them: the bank or supermarket, a parking slot. I remember a special case in a company where I worked. We had an assistant for a team of professionals, whose job was to produce the documents in the appropriate format. I had the responsibility, among other things, to collect the documents to be produced and took them to the assistant. She arrived in the morning and sat down to read a novel. When I needed the production of any document, I took it to her and she did it as soon as possible to continue reading. For months we never had a delay with any document, until the assistant had to leave a couple of weeks. Her replacement arrived earlier and she was always busy. When I was going to ask her for a document, she gave reasons to explain why it was going to take hours or days, because she had a lot of work. How we missed the novel of the first one!

So, it is not true that being busy is to be productive.

If being idle is considered to be wrong, the resulting contradiction generates conflicts to the people and the system, leading to anti systemic decisions, causing costly errors.

The fundamental error of the 20th century (and part of 21st) is to ignore the systemic nature of the companies.

In the following chapters, I will go reeling off all the negative ramifications that this error has in each of the activities of the companies.

Dr. Goldratt expressed this error otherwise. In the very specific case of production, he said that the error was considering all idle resource as a waste. This is a derivation of the more general assumption mentioned above, which consists in ignoring that organizations are systems.

The Fundamental Solution: a Change of Era

If the fundamental error is to ignore the systemic nature of companies, it is obvious that the solution is to recognize that businesses are systems, so that a systemic design to manage them should give a better result. Not only better, but superior in any aspect to be measured.

The idea of change of era was taken from Dr. Russell L. Ackoff (12 February 1919 - 29 October 2009), who was one of the pioneers in applying the systems approach to organizations. Graduated in 1941 from the University of Pennsylvania as architect, he enlisted in the United States Navy and was stationed in front of the Philippines in the II World War. In 1946 he returned to study at the same University and obtained his doctorate in Philosophy of Science in 1947.

His academic career, and in consulting afterwards, it was shaping up with the idea that organizations are systems. Ackoff was one of the first authors to write about the Operations Research, incorporating mathematical models for solving complex problems in companies.

In my case, studying civil engineering at the Catholic University of Chile in the 80s, I studied the techniques of operations research, with special emphasis on the mathematical models known as linear and non-linear programming. Now I understand what they were about such models, when I more deeply understood the systems approach. At that time I didn't see the relationship between the models and looking at companies as systems. Neither it was part of the explicit explanations.

Out of university and beginning to work, I never saw that even one manager would mention a mathematical programming model to make decisions. In one occasion I built a model to better understand how to optimize the production of a factory where I was the export manager. I had to leave it because it was consuming time and did not come to clear conclusions. The main reason for this is clear now: the parameters of the functions that were involved in my model had extensive ranges of variation. Something told me that I was going in the right direction but the first talks with the production manager convinced me that I would not go too far with that approach. It was too complex to solve a problem that in the company seemed to be already resolved. I had problems in my area, but did not have the support to find mathematical solutions for them.

Years later, when I was getting a better understanding of the Goldratt Theory, I understood that my naive attempt to model the production had a systemic basis; and that collided head-on with the prevailing culture in that company. To that anti-systemic culture Goldratt use to call it the "cost world". We will see in the following chapters the contrast between the two cultures and how the cost world prevails in management education and so is perpetuated in the companies, and it is just another way to call the fundamental error already described[7].

Going back to Dr. Ackoff, he also suffered disappointments when he saw that his developments in mathematical models were understood as a technique, but not as a fundamental change in vision.

---

[7] The annex contains a simplified exercise to highlight the difference between the decisions of the "world of cost" and the decisions of the "world of throughput".

Dr. Ackoff was a pioneer in the development of operations research, as already mentioned, where the mathematical models take the system as a whole, which led him to be one of the best exponents to apply systems thinking to organizations. He wrote 35 books and over 250 articles, where there are many texts explaining how organizations are systems and should be treated as such.

The friendship between Ackoff and Peter Drucker was forged very early in the life of both, and Drucker recognized to Ackoff the critical contributions to his work. Ackoff treasured a letter of Drucker, sent a couple of years before the death of the latter, where he said:

> *I was then, as you may recall, one of the early ones who applied Operations Research and the new methods of Quantitative Analysis to specific BUSINESS PROBLEMS—rather than, as they had been originally developed for, to military or scientific problems. I had led teams applying the new methodology in two of the world's largest companies—GE and AT&T. We had successfully solved several major production and technical problems for these companies—and my clients were highly satisfied. But I was not—we had solved TECHNICAL problems but our work had no impact on the organizations and on their mindsets. On the contrary: we had all but convinced the managements of these two big companies that QUANTITATIVE MANIPULATION was a substitute for THINKING. And then your work and your example showed us—or at least, it showed me—that the QUANTITATIVE ANALYSIS comes AFTER the THINKING—it validates the thinking; it shows up intellectual sloppiness and uncritical reliance on precedent, on untested assumptions and on the seemingly "obvious." But it does not substitute for hard, rigorous, intellectually challenging THINKING. It demands it, though—but does not replace it. This is, of course, what YOU mean BY system. And your work in those far-away days thus saved me—as it saved countless others—from either descending into mindless "model building" – the disease that all*

but destroyed so many of the Business Schools in the last decades—or from sloppiness parading as 'insight.'[8]

Ackoff was one of the major drivers of systemic thinking, that came to assert that we are living through a change of era, because the assumptions that we share about our vision of reality, shared culturally for a long time, are changing. In particular, the vision of what an organization is, how it works, and what it produces, is changing gradually from a mechanical to a systemic vision. [9]

Like any change of era, it faces resistance from the establishment and it takes effort for people to question their deepest beliefs, especially when they have given sustenance to so many decisions of the past. Let us not forget that self-esteem comes, in a large part, from the satisfaction for the good decisions that we make. And this change of culture might make it appear that many managers wasted years of their own and their companies. To subtract drama to this reflection I will quote to my mentor and friend, Eli Goldratt: "I won't apologize for not having invented something before." Equally, there is no reason to be frustrated to see that many of the beliefs learned at the university, shared with managers within and outside of the company itself, and considered the basis for "best practices", were wrong. Learning is often a beliefs destructor.

Progress has always been a history of replacing one knowledge on the other. Schumpeter called it creative destruction. As we shall see later, one of the principles of Goldratt is that knowledge is unlimited, and I conclude that what we know is nothing compared with what we do not know.

Perhaps it is a matter of frustration if one resists a change for inertia or for social pressure, or for worse reasons. If being able to understand the change and its positive consequences, one decides to take refuge in the comfort, obstructing the progress of many by omission. Such an attitude, to me, would bring a great discomfort in

---

[8] Letter of Peter Drucker to Russell Ackoff circa 2003. It appears in the book Managing for the Next Society by Peter Drucker (2002), in the prologue written by Alistair Mant and Cary L. Cooper for the 2007 edition.

[9] From mechanistic to social systemic thinking, Russell L. Ackoff, 1984, January 18, (11/93 Systems Thinking in Action Conference).

hindsight. It is a profound unrest that comes from shirking the own responsibility when acting against the ethics that clearly shows me the good that I should pursue, even if it means effort and resignation. Effort to promote the necessary actions. Resignation of beliefs that accompanied me until that moment, and which were the basis for decisions of the past, which also leads to renunciation of that image of infallible that we like to boast sometimes.

In his book Futuro-Presente[10], Alfredo Barriga shows us how a digital revolution is coming to change our lives. It is fascinating to see how paradigms are changing with new technologies. And as I read this book, I better understand how the cultural change that I am talking about here can further enhance the benefits that Alfredo is speaking about.

When the majority of the managers adopt the systemic thinking and accept the principles of Goldratt to think clearly[11], I believe that we will see a change of era enhanced with all the other technologies that are changing our world. But a change of era characterized not so much by the greater material well-being, which by the way will come, but by the greater harmony in the social fabric. I will go deeper about it in the following chapters.

The Contribution of Dr. Eliyahu Goldratt

I already talked about the mathematical models of operations research, which are complex, and they also have the limitations of a model, which simplifies aspects of reality. And being the reality of companies so complex, it is impractical to try to make decisions using these models, despite the fact that I learned them in my degree in engineering, and they continue to teach them.

The fundamental concept of these mathematical programming models is that a system has a measurable purpose, which is represented by an objective function, which is a formula

---

[10] Futuro Presente: Cómo la nueva revolución digital afectará mi vida (Spanish Edition) (Spanish) Paperback – September 21, 2016, Alfredo Barriga, https://www.amazon.com/Futuro-Presente-revoluci%C3%B3n-digital-afectar%C3%A1/dp/9563628454

[11] See "The Choice", E.M.Goldratt, 2008.

that tells us how much value the system is generating to the extent that delivers units of what it produces. For example, if we produce two products that we can call P and Q, where each unit of P generates a gross margin of $45, and each unit of Q generates $60, then our function to maximize would be 45*P+60*Q.

And that formula or function would have an infinite result if it not were that we have limitations of time and perhaps of other resources, without forgetting that the market is not infinite and also puts limitations. These limitations are called constraints and can also be represented as functions. For example, if we say that every unit of P consumes 15 minutes of a resource, and that each unit of Q consumes 10 minutes of the same resource, and we know that the resource is available 40 hours a week (this is 2400 minutes), then we can represent the constraint as 15*P+ 10*Q ≤ 2400 for one week. We can do the same thing with all the resources involved.

Then our model will say something like: we want to maximize our objective function subject to a set of constraints that are represented by functions such as those described.

Even this example with two products and, say, only four resources, is not easy to solve mathematically. And when we solve it, we discover that some resources actually used completely their capacity and we call them active constraints, and the others are idle for several minutes in the week, and are non-active constraints.

The capacity of the system to generate value is limited by the constraints. However, as I said above, the value is generated by the interactions of all parties, so that all resources are essential, whether active constraints or not.

The genius of Goldratt, who was a physicist, (and physicists are good mathematicians but don't get caught by the mathematical theory but seek the practical application), said something very simple. In each system, for practical purposes, the constraints are very few and do not change frequently over time.

In this more detailed explanation of what has already expressed earlier in this chapter, there is a detail that now is relevant to understand why the contribution of Goldratt is so valuable.

If one takes the preceding example and identifies in advance which is the resource that will be the active constraint, the mathematical problem is much easier to solve. But this is not what the experts in operations research do.

The year 2004 I took part as a lecturer and as an attendant in several lectures of the International Conference for Production Research[12], where I met with an old acquaintance: my professor of mathematical programming. He was presenting a model that included two generic models, which interacted among themselves. He told us that he had run the model in a company several hundreds of times and that the resulting decisions had increased profits. I expected no less, after all I said that these models are systemic. When we get to the questions I raise my hand to ask if they had done a statistical study of which constraints had been active each time. I caught him by surprise with the question, and he had not done so. But then he asked me why would I want to do that. My response was that if the active constraints were always a few and the same, that would greatly simplify the model, with which he agreed but expressed serious doubts as to whether that was possible.

I am sure that at universities they still believe in highly complex models, hard to sell to a group of managers and finally, as Drucker said, distract you from what is really important: use your mind to think clearly. For this type of things Goldratt spoke of the "stupid admiration for sophistication", by which was not very popular, neither before nor now. It is no surprise then that the gap between the prevailing practice anti-systemic and too sophisticated systemic models, remains open. The necessary change is a cultural one.

This idea of Goldratt was captured in a process that he wrote in a night out with friends in a napkin. I was not a witness of this great moment, but Eli himself told it to me, so I hope to be faithful to the story.

---

[12] ICPR AMERICAS`2004, Agosto 1-4, 2004, Santiago, Chile

He was fresh out of Creative Output, the company that he had co-founded shortly before, with a great sorrow because he had been misunderstood and there were unsurmountable disagreements with other partners. This story reminds me of what Drucker told Ackoff in the letter quoted before. With the software that had been created in Creative Output, the results of the companies had improved a lot. But it was in productivity, and the leap was so big that the pressure on marketing and sales was immense, to the point that they resisted. The companies were then with a lot of idle capacity, and converted the improvement in money by reducing staff[13]. Goldratt tried to explain to them that this was going against the system, which should continue to improve without anyone to suffer for it. He came to propose to its partners that the company will no longer sell the software and make another thing, which led them to ask for his resignation.

In his words, he would sacrifice nobody for his goal in life, but neither would accept that others would force him to sacrifice his goal. And he agreed to withdraw the company (I guess that with some financial arrangement that never asked him... it was not the important issue).

And he was in the formation of what would be the Goldratt Institute when, in one of those nights, took a napkin and wrote what he called the Process of Ongoing Improvement. These are the five steps[14]:

- Identify the constraint of the system.
- Decide how to exploit the constraint of the system.
- Subordinate everything else to the previous decision.
- Elevate the constraint of the system.
- Go back to step 1[15].

---

[13] In that time they used euphemisms for this anti-systemic action: rationalizing, downsizing, adjusting, etc.
[14] Here they are reproduced as I believe that he originally wrote them. The wording was refined afterwards.
[15] Afterwards, in the book The Goal, he added a warning to this step.

These five steps are equivalent to apply mathematical models of optimization in a very practical and simple way. And it constitutes the first documented tool of Theory of Constraints or TOC[16].

But this is not all. Goldratt not only made efforts to resolve a technical problem, and nothing more. What he did was to face every inconsistency in the administration of companies and he went designing solutions to eliminate them. And to explain this and to develop more knowledge, he invented some mental artifacts that he called Thinking Processes. These are three logical tools with a variety of uses [17]. And to the extent required, invented other processes also: to extract maximum value from new technologies and innovations, or how to design an effective persuasive communication, and a few more.

Today the Theory of Constraints is a solid body of knowledge, which is based on the four principles that Goldratt established to think clearly:

- Every system, as complex as it can be, contains an inherent simplicity.
- Every conflict (or contradiction) can be removed.
- Do not blame people[18].
- Never say I know.

And on the basis of the principles and applying the tools, many systemic applications have been developed. In the following chapters I will show the problems generated by the anti-systemic approach and how these applications are the solution in each case.

In my opinion, the contribution of Goldratt

---

[16] Years later I learned from Goldratt that in Bar Ilan University he had devised a few trees, but he used them again from the 2004, but this process of improvement was the first that formally belongs to TOC - Theory of Constraints, the theory created by Goldratt.

[17] The Cloud, the Logical Branch, the Pre-Requisite Tree.

[18] Goldratt formulated it as "people are good," but I prefer this that prevents a value judgment and it's more of a principle of action.

> *is huge for having created this body of knowledge that allows the implementation of the systems thinking in a very practical way, even in the more complex systems.*

I do not want to omit something that seems to me to be very relevant. The consensus on adopting a systemic approach is very broad. It is even difficult to find managers who deny that their companies are systems or scholars who are avowedly anti systemic. This fact leads me to ask, why its adoption is not massive?

My answer is that to understand something and being able to apply it are far from being the same. In particular in the universities, in Engineering and in Business Administration, or even Economics, it is not explicitly presented that companies are systems, i.e., entities that are distinct from its constituent parts, and whose purpose is achieved by the interaction between the parts and not as the sum of the actions of each part. And from there, with separate courses of production, logistics, projects, marketing, strategy, etc., there is the impression that one is learning how to manage a company. Quoting Russell Ackoff, that is nonsense: as much you learn production, logistics, or marketing, but not to manage the whole, which is the company.

And specifically, there are several groups and entities that have promoted and promote the systemic approach. An example is the SDM - MIT[19], the master's degree program in engineering from the Massachusetts Institute of Technology. It's called Systems Design and Management. They have an annual conference where they meet to present research and application papers. There is enough material available in documents and videos from the proceedings to get an idea of what they are developing.

Another is Peter Checkland from Lancaster University in England. Professor Checkland is considered the creator of SSM[20], soft systems management, to differentiate them from "hard" systems

---

[19] https://sdm.mit.edu/
[20] SSM: Soft Systems Management.

such as a car.

Peter Senge has been a promoter of the systemic thinking when writing in his book "The Fifth Discipline" that systemic thinking is the fifth discipline that articulates the other four that he mentioned as necessary to manage companies. In his lectures, he always articulates his speeches around the idea of interdependence and of systems.

John Seddon, creator of the Vanguard Method, applies systems thinking to service companies. Without knowing in detail the tools and methods of Vanguard, I think that it is one of the most practical and simple that I have known.

Of course all the work of Russell Ackoff, one of the greatest exponents of systemic thinking.

On the internet you can find many groups dedicated to promoting systemic thinking.

The consensus is broad: it requires a systemic approach to manage our organizations, in particular companies.

However, knowing what I know, it will be very difficult that managers can apply these ideas with the tools presented by these groups. I even think that they try to apply the systems approach with the wrong principles. For example, I have a document stating that there is no such thing as a simple solution to a complex problem. If one really believes in the above statement, will never put the effort to think until the simplicity that exists in any complex system is found.

As a counterexample refutes a claim, we will see how all the solutions designed by Goldratt are simple solutions to complex problems.

This leads us to the fact that in the world of systemic thinkers, being in agreement with the definition and the need to apply it to companies, there is no agreement on how to do it.

I repeat it once more: the contribution of Goldratt is immense because he has built up a body of knowledge that allows the simple and practical application of the systemic approach. What is more, he established the principles for any application of the systemic approach.

I think that a good analogy to understand what I mean is that the Goldratt Theory is to the systemic approach as the differential calculus is to physics: not only it can be better understood, but its applications create real value for each specific case.

LEAN: Enemy N° 2 of Productivity

Toyota Production System

In the decade of 1930, Kiichiro Toyoda took over the company founded by his father Sakichi. It was a weaving devices factory called Toyoda Automatic Loom Works, in the city of Nagoya. Eiji Toyoda, a cousin of Kiichiro, finished his studies of mechanical engineering in 1936 and joined the company. In 1938, Kiichiro asked his cousin Eiji to oversee the construction of a new plant in the nearby town of Koromo, to enter the automotive manufacturing, which came to be known as Toyota City. Until today, this plant is known as the mothership of Toyota Corporation.

Kiichiro resigned from the presidency of the company in 1950 due to low sales. Just at that time, Eiji visited one of the Ford plants in Michigan, where he was highly impressed with the mass production. Toyota had produced a little more than 2500 cars in 13 years, while at the Ford plant they produced 8000 vehicles per day. In 1957, Eiji was named president of the company, whose name already was Toyota.

Eiji Toyoda returned with plans to achieve in Toyota productions as he saw in Ford. For that, he sought the collaboration of one of the former machinists in the looms factory, Taiichi Ohno.

Taiichi Ohno is considered the father of the Toyota Production System. Ohno was referring to his system as a river system, meaning that what they did was to facilitate the flow of products from the raw material to the customers.

I do not know if you, dear reader, have already noticed the systemic nature of the concept of Ohno. According to this concept, which each part does is only important in the whole of the river and not separately.

Robert Fox, a close associate of Goldratt in 1990, wrote his experience of a meeting that the three, Ohno, Goldratt and himself had in a hotel room in Chicago, where they exchanged ideas[21].

At that meeting, Ohno said the following things[22]:

We needed to make such improvements on many types of machines. The biggest obstacle was not in finding ways to change over the machines quickly. It was in convincing our managers and workers that they should operate in this fashion. Once someone finished setting up a machine, they wanted to produce as many parts as possible -that was the efficient way. I had many struggles to persuade people that it may be efficient for that machine, but it was very inefficient for my river system[23].

I have heard many people say that the Japanese are special, and that is why they find it easy to understand these concepts of systemic thinking. Ohno did not felt the same.

Making my river system flow smoothly and rapidly took nearly 40 years of continued, incremental improvement[24].

When asked how he did it, grinning, he responded:

---

[21] Profitability with No Boundaries, Reza Pirasteh y Robert Fox, 2015.
[22] The quotes are taken from the quoted book, where they appear as literal quotes from the meeting.
[23] Ibíd.
[24] Ibíd.

I used a gun! I literally would shoot people if they didn't follow my direction. It was brutal, but eventually it worked[25].

We have a joke in TOC. How many consultants of TOC are required to change a light bulb? Only one, but the light bulb must want to be changed! Ohno tried another way to persuade.

Another myth: we must reach consensus to have results. In practice I do believe in this, because the greatest wealth of the company will come from the collaboration and commitment of its people. But in the beginning of a change, I see no problem in forcing the actions for a week or two, until you see results. Here it comes the time of the explanations and consensus.

If we believe that consensus is absolutely necessary before taking the first actions, we will have a lot of problems and "we will confirm" that people have resistance to change and that a process of "paradigm shift" is very difficult.

Of course that a history of 40 years can lead to such a conclusion, but in my experience, the changes that have immediate impact can be made with a minimum of consensus and fast forward to the next, with the momentum that is created when you get the first visible results.

And why Ohno took so much?

My first hypothesis is that, despite the fact that they were inspired by something that had already worked, the assembly line at Ford, the circumstances were not the same, so that the same techniques of Ford did not work well for Toyota. See the article by Dr. Goldratt about the evolution from Ford, to the TPS, to TOC[26].

Ohno had to go inventing and overcoming obstacles. With regard to obstacles, Goldratt was made popular by his famous phrase "cost accounting is the enemy number 1 of productivity". The

---

[25] Ibíd.
[26] "Standing on the Shoulders of Giants", Goldratt, 2008. An internet search first displays the fourth studio album of Oasis, then the attribution of the phrase to Newton, for the same reasons that Goldratt titled so his article. If you add "GOLDRATT" to the search, you get the full text of the article.

reason for that is that the systemic nature of a company implies that the value is generated by the interactions between the parts. And cost accounting takes into account each part separately, as if it did not belong to the system, which produces a dissociation of the calculated costs from the system's primary objective, which is to generate value.

Goldratt and Fox asked Ohno: "How do cost accountants think in Japan? Do they believe strongly in local efficiencies, in making large batches to save setups and things like that?"

When the question was translated, Ohno stirred a lot and a red color in his neck began to surface to the point that Goldratt and Fox were uncomfortable for having offended his illustrious interlocutor. But as they heard the translated response of Ohno, they realized that, on the contrary, it was mutual sympathy they could feel with each other. Ohno said:

> *You have touched my rawest nerve. The cost accountants in Japan think just like they do in the Western world. They believe in all those things you mentioned and many more that are at odds with my river system. These beliefs were the biggest obstacle I had to overcome*[27].

And to the question of how did he overcome this huge obstacle, Ohno replied:

> *First I kept the cost accountants out of my plants, but I found that was not a solution. I needed to keep these ideas out of the minds of my people. It wasn't the cost accountants that were the problem, but all of these ideas about the efficiency of an operation. They were contrary to my desire to create an efficient system. I spent many years trying to persuade people to think differently, but without much success*[28].

The book that you have in your hands has as main objective to persuade all the decision-makers to adopt the systemic thinking as the framework of analysis for all that is system: companies,

---

[27] Profitability with No Boundaries, Reza Pirasteh y Robert Fox, 2015.
[28] Ibíd.

organizations in general, countries. I hope that some will open their mind and examine the logic of reasoning, in spite of their old beliefs.

And once again we see that the assertion of Ohno could confirm that profound changes are very complicated. However, and relying on the third principle of TOC, I believe that people will never resist an improvement, and the greater part of the difficulty in persuasion should be attributed to the person who persuades.

Returning to our little story, Goldratt and Fox showed Ohno the mechanism to facilitate the flow designed by Goldratt, which was described in detail in his most famous novel[29]. After some questions and answers, Ohno studied the diagrams that they had drawn along with the explanations, in silence, and then said:

> **If I had seen this possibility I believe I could have developed my system in less than half the time[30].**

With this statement from the same Ohno, creator of the TPS, which is today considered one of the greatest achievements in manufacturing, I can say that it is worthwhile to understand how TOC is a body of knowledge more simple for the implementation of systemic thinking. And not only that, for the implementation of systemic thinking in all aspects of a company, not only in their operations.

LEAN Manufacturing: a provoked confusion

I guess I have demonstrated my admiration for Taiichi Ohno and for the TPS (Toyota Production System).

You will recall that paragraphs above I said that Ohno and Toyoda were trying to emulate Ford, and that they encountered many difficulties to use the same techniques that Ford used.

For example, Ford achieved a very efficient system to produce the Ford Model T, in black, because it did not produce

---
[29] The Goal, Goldratt, 1984.
[30] Profitability with No Boundaries, Reza Pirasteh y Robert Fox, 2015.

anything else. And part of his system was to paint areas on the floor of his plant to limit the production of parts that are not needed immediately. If the area was full, they could not continue assembling that part, and that resource should stop.

Toyota, after 1950, needed to produce several different models, so the idea of painting the floor was not good. But he needed to limit the production, as well as Ford, and used the inventory. So it arose the idea of the cards, or *kanban*.

The TPS was slow to develop, and it looks different to the assembly line at Ford, but both share the same philosophy to make material flow.

Ohno studied his system and went making the changes that removed obstacles to the flow; he did not copy methods or techniques.

When there was interest in knowing more about the success of Toyota, there were groups of visitors from different parts of the United States and Europe. Ohno describes these visits:

> *I'm proud to be Japanese and I wanted my country to succeed. I believed my system was a way that could help us become a modern industrial nation. That is why I had no problem with sharing it with other Japanese companies, even my biggest competitors. But I was very, very concerned that you Americans and the Europeans would understand what we were doing, copy it, and defeat us in the marketplace[31].*

After saying that he continued telling that when American and European came to Toyota, he went out of his way to confuse them about why Toyota was so successful. This is what he said:

> *I explained it by talking about techniques, like quicker machine setups, reduction of the seven wastes (muda), and other techniques with Japanese names like kanban and kaizen. I did my best to prevent the visitors from fully grasping our overall approach. Today I am ready to be open and explain fully what we*

---
[31] Ibid.

did. We are now strong enough to deal with any competition[32].

And what was what they understood the ones that went there? I remember my years in engineering at the Catholic University of Chile, where they explained us the JIT system - just in time of the Japanese. I never heard a word about a system or a river. Years later I saw how they changed the name to Lean Manufacturing. Please, do an internet search for these words.

I just did that search and found many sites that describe "lean manufacturing" as the set of tools to reduce the seven wastes in manufacturing.

That is to say, Ohno was so successful that even today there is all this confusion.

Do you think that I am exaggerating with confusion?

This is a quote from an article published by the LEAN Institute explaining the TPS:

(LEAN is) A production system steeped in the philosophy of "the complete elimination of all waste", permeating all aspects of production in the search for the most efficient methods[33].

I don't see there the philosophy of the Ohno river system, rather I see the reduction of waste.

To illustrate the point, let me tell you a very recent story.

In April of 2017, I was on a visit of implementation in a plant in Lima. Looking at the system as a river I already had the perception that we needed to do something just after the cut of material. And there was the coincidence that the internal processes team, led by a Lean expert, also had the idea to improve that part of the process.

The case is that they are cutting between six and ten

---

[32] Ibíd..
[33] http://www.institutolean.org/index.php/es/acerca-de/que-es-lean/73-tps-toyota-production-system

components for each piece that must be assembled later, but a minority of these components requires a process that can take between six and seventy-two additional hours. This causes most of the components take up space, which is scarce, while waiting for the other components, preventing the cutting of components in the days that followed.

As I see it, those components that wait are blocking the flow, in addition to being damaged and lost.

But the Lean expert is concerned with reducing the processing time in that part of the process. He wants to reduce waste.

If they run the Lean project, this is going to cause more problems to the flow, and it's going to be an obstacle to the implementation of TOC that I am leading. I am in the process of communication so that they do not make mistakes of applying techniques without looking at the system as a whole[34].

I have many stories similar to this one in more than a decade of implementing TOC, in industries as diverse as manufacturing of steel cables, stickers or financial services for micro businesses, among others.

Unfortunately I have also known stories where you try to implement a technique of TOC without studying the system. That is to say, the problem are not the methods. The problem is the mentality with which they are applied. Ohno could have failed if he had copied to Ford, as many have failed trying to copy the TPS or successful implementations of TOC.

As I said in the first chapter, the fundamental error that prevails in most economies today is not to consider the systemic nature of the companies.

---

[34] As it was expected, we agreed on the global objective, and it didn't take too much to reach an agreement on what actions were the best.

And having been the TPS so successful, one believes that there is not much to contribute to that system, and draws the erroneous conclusion that we will be better if we apply it as it is.

To understand me well, I must make it clear that I have seen Lean experts who have understood what Ohno did, and they propose to study the system and plan for the improvement with the river system in mind. And here is where analysis tools such as the Kata of improvement have its place:

- Understand the direction.
- Capture current condition.
- Establish next target condition.
- PDCA[35] towards the next target condition.

And only when we know what we want to improve, we will see what waste is blocking the flow.

With regard to the seven wastes, and bearing in mind that we want to improve the flow through the system, I have these comments:

- Overproduction: I totally agree, is the main obstacle to the flow when an excess of work-in-process (WIP) is allowed.
- Inventory: another way to express the first one.
- Waiting: here I have a problem. If this is a waste that we should reduce, we will try to balance the capacity of each work center. The balancing of a line destroys the flow through the dependent resources with statistical fluctuations. You will find more details about this in the chapter of operations. The key is to synchronize. For the next resource to quickly process the material, it's the resource which must wait, not the material. This is not a waste in most cases.
- Motion: this may or may not block the flow. In the story that I told of the plant in Lima, this is one of the wastes that they try to eliminate. It is not always better

---

[35] PDCA: plan-do-check-act. Tool design by Shrewart and perfected by Deming.

- to eliminate certain motions. Sometimes the flow improved by adding some additional motions.
- Transport: the same as the previous. It depends on the circumstances.
- Defects: I agree, this is a great waste. Ironically the reduction of waiting or motion generates more defects most of the times.
- Over-processing: I agree; it should not be processed nothing more than what is required. But still I have seen occasions where to remove this waste can block the flow. For example, if I have two batches that can fit on a kiln, one of the batches requires 10 hours and the other requires 6 hours, and the second is equally well finished with 10 hours, I would make them together. If I want to eliminate the second "overprocess", I am adding hours of waiting to one of the batches, without gaining anything.

Typically, a Lean expert is going to study the system and he'll find many sources of waste. Then he'll open improvement projects for each of these opportunities and to improve the system. If we're lucky, they will not block the flow with some of these projects, however it will divert resources. In the worst of cases, some of these projects will block the flow in ways so subtle that it is difficult to detect.

We will see in the chapter about operations that it is necessary to have idle capacity in the system to facilitate the flow. Balancing capacities of resources leads to reduce the combined capacity of the system. That is to say, more capacity in most of the resources, controlled accumulation of in-progress inventory and waiting times of resources are required to facilitate the flow. These slacks are what in TOC are called buffers.

The confusion is to consider waste any needed buffers to facilitate the flow. Removing the buffers blocks the flow.

Because of this confusion, still prevailing in much of the Lean community, is that I affirm that Lean, poorly understood, as a means of waste reduction, is the enemy number 2 of productivity. The number 1, let us not forget, is cost accounting.

LEAN and 6-Sigma techniques well utilized

Everything that was said for Lean can be applied to 6-Sigma, which is another set of tools for improvement. In this case is not to reduce waste but to reduce variability.

We will see in the chapter about operations all the detail of how to manage a flow with dependent resources. I will anticipate that it is necessary to have buffers to protect the flow due to the variability. The buffers are interchangeable and can be more capacity, more time or more inventory, as already mentioned.

If I reduce waste of time in an operation that is active constraint, the total system capacity increases. This is real improvement.

If I reduce the variability of the system, the total WIP needed to take advantage of the capacity can be reduced, thereby reducing the cycle time. This is also an improvement.

When the system is in the process of governing with systemic thinking and the TOC philosophy, improvement projects are always few and focused where you can improve the flow. And the same mechanisms of control highlight opportunities for improvement. But the vast majority of the opportunities for improvement in every part of the system do not improve the flow, thus they do damage instead for diverting resources in what is not needed at that time.

Systemic Approach in Operations

Introduction

The first thing that Dr. Goldratt did when jumping from the university to the business world was to analyze a productive process to find a way to schedule the production with finite capacity in a manufacturing company of Israel.

It was 1978 and there were several initiatives with this idea, but the algorithm of Goldratt is the only one who succeeded in achieving a plan that would allow the control of the execution to the extent of predicting, with some accuracy, what would happen and on what dates.

In a factory is not very important if one proposes an elegant model; the important thing is to get results. Dr. Goldratt obtained them and, with other people, he founded a company to offer this algorithm. The company was Creative Output and offered the software OPT (Optimized Production Timetables).

After a while implementing, this software proved to give very good results in production. This in itself was an achievement. But it introduced a pressure on the rest of the company that generated problems, for this reason Dr. Goldratt decided that they should provide a systemic vision for the entire company and not only production, which meant irreconcilable differences with his partners.

This chapter will cover how to apply systems thinking to the "production system". In fact we will see that the principles to manage a flow are valid for production, projects, distribution and support functions.

You can identify a primary value chain, from design, supply of raw materials, production and delivery of products, including the case where production occurs within a project. And this primary chain is fed with different inputs from support functions such as production of documents (technical, contractual, commercial), quality control, maintenance, technical service, and there may be others.

The principles of flow that we'll see apply to both the primary and secondary chains, but we will see the differences of application in each case.

I have seen in many companies, the results of the fundamental error in all these functions, both primary and secondary. And when we have corrected it, the results are quick and forceful.

And when we delay in correct it, despite all the explanations and agreements, actions take time to run properly and the results take too long to arrive.

Principles of Flow

Dr. Goldratt applied his logic first to determine an algorithm in 1978. After that he generalized the process developing the method that called Drum-Buffer-Rope[36] between 1982 and 1984, and in 2008 he published an article where he offered a review of the Ford assembly line and the Toyota Production System, on the grounds that in both cases they applied the same principles.

---

[36] The name of this method comes from an analogy that Dr. Goldratt used to explain it. It was a company of soldiers who were marching to the beat of a drum, tied with a rope that was allowed to a greater length which it was the buffer.

The 2008 article entitled "Standing on the Shoulders of Giants"[37] , using the well-known expression centuries ago attributed to Newton and other celebrities.

This article shows how the Ford assembly line was so successful because it is not allowed to accumulate excess material between each one of the work centers. Ford painted on the floor the areas where they could put the processed parts. If there was no space, operators could not continue processing while pieces did not move making room for new ones.

This method works very well when the product is unique. It is known the phrase of Ford when he said that he offered the Ford Model T in any color that was black.

Taichi Ohno, the engineer who worked with Toyoda developing the TPS[38], studied that assembly line and wanted to replicate the success of Ford, but he encountered the difficulty of the large variability in the models, on demand, in the resources load. He quickly realized that he could not use the space to control the material in the process. He decided to use the inventory and the result was the now famous KANBAN[39].

Ohno took 15 to 20 years to achieve the stability of that system because it requires reducing the variability to values within narrow ranges. For example, each change of model required an average of 8 hours in some work centers. He had to develop SMED[40] to reduce that time to a matter of minutes.

Dr. Goldratt realized that both Ford and Ohno had developed a method to control the flow based on controlling the work in progress or WIP. And that he had done the same, but using

---

[37] Standing on the shoulders of giants, E. Goldratt, 2008.
[38] TPS Toyota Production System
[39] KANBAN is the Japanese word for card. Each work center has a maximum quantity of parts that can accumulate. When it is asked for parts already processed, it sends a card to the previous work center to replenish material to process and replace the parts delivered.
[40] SMED: Single-Minute Exchange of Die. This method distinguishes the tasks that can be done with the machine running (external setup) and those that require full stop (internal setup). Intelligence is applied to the latter to reduce the time.

the time instead of the physical space or inventory.

There are several advantages of using the time: it does not require inventory produced in advance, it allows much greater flexibility in product mix, there are no constraints to the flow between the work centers, allowing for greater variability in loads, and several others.

As already mentioned, on the occasion that Dr. Ohno had the opportunity to talk with Dr. Goldratt, Ohno felt that the time to achieve the same results would have reduced to less than half if he had thought the solution that Goldratt explained.

In the quoted article, Dr. Goldratt exposes the four principles of flow that he deduced from this study:

1. Improving flow (or equivalently lead time) is a primary objective of operations.
2. This primary objective should be translated into a practical mechanism that guides the operation when not to produce (prevents overproduction).
3. Local efficiencies must be abolished.
4. A focusing process to balance flow must be in place.

These four principles have profound consequences because they contradict many myths that are still accepted in industries and universities.

That is, these principles are correct only if the following statements are false:

- Any idle time in production is a waste.
- The sooner I start something, the sooner I finish it.
- Reducing unit cost of a product (calculated with cost accounting) reduces actual cost.

There may be other similar beliefs that also contradict these principles, and for this reason it's why adopting systemic thinking is a profound cultural change, which is not yet general.

Managing a flow

Uncertainty

To manage a flow there are two basic activities, and we will use flow principles to design each specific application:

- Planning or programming the flow
- Controlling the flow

Whenever I ask managers why they have production or project plans, the answers point to having control of the process. And I agree with this, that's why the second activity is flow control.

We agree on the objectives, but almost never agree on the actions or tactics to achieve them. A widespread belief is "the more detail in the planning, the more control in the execution".

And this belief is manifested in detailed production programs by machine and by day, even some put hours. Or in projects, a project planning with very detailed tasks, with estimated durations of hours. Or consumption forecasts to plan inventories that go to the level of product, store and for several days. Or the well-known annual budgets of expenses and income by areas in the companies.

Uncertainty is part of reality. The more detailed the plan is, the greater the variability with which each part is exposed to, therefore, the percentage errors of estimation are greater.

For example, if I intend to program the successive processes of a production order, where each process has an estimated duration of 30 minutes, but which can be 15 minutes or sometimes 120 minutes, it is most likely that the second unit, or the second process , do not comply with the plan. The same applies to tasks in projects, budgets and inventories.

Each time an aggregation is made, the percentage error is reduced. If we roll a die once, we can get between 1 and 6, with an average of 3.5 (which is not a possible result). If we throw 10 times, the average of the sum is 35, and the probable extremes of this sum are closer to the average than in the case of a single throw. That is, when I throw once, I can make a mistake in +2.5 or -2.5, which is a 70% error up or down. But if I throw ten times, the probable extremes are not 10 and 60, surely they are much closer to 30 and 40, leading to an error of less than 30%.

This reduction of the error by aggregation can be achieved by adding up units (families of products instead of individual products), time (lengthening the time of the estimate), population. They are all equivalent: if one is made, the other is achieved.

When planning the flow is done at a very detailed level, it contains so much error that there really is no control. One knows that this is true when is forced to reprogram. Every time I have to reprogram, I must admit that I lost control and I want to recover it.

> **The first element of good programming is having an adequate amount of aggregation.**

WIP Control

On the other hand, the second principle of flow says that overproduction must be avoided.

Why should overproduction be avoided? To Ford, Ohno and Goldratt it turned out! Do we need more explanation?

I believe we do; we need to understand well what this second principle means and we need to understand why it is effective to know how to apply it well in each case.

I will begin by appealing to your intuition. I think it is safe to assume that you have been on the highway more than once, and that you can usually move at a speed close to the maximum and other times you have been forced to go much slower.

On the occasions that should have been very slow, assuming that it is against your will, I dare to assume that it was when there were many more cars on the road. This is the most generic case of traffic jams in addition to an accident.

Note that an accident disables one or two tracks in a stretch, which reduces the actual flow capacity.

When there is a traffic jam without an accident, the speed is very similar but none of the tracks was unused. What happened there? It is a phenomenon known many years ago by traffic engineers, and models to estimate the capacity of a road in terms of vehicles per hour, take into account the density of vehicles per kilometer. They have a maximum flow for a certain density and that flow rate begins to decrease for higher densities.

In other systems, similar phenomena occur. In queuing theory the phenomenon is also described, when the demand exceeds 90% of the capacity, the queue grows exponentially, increasing the time and reducing the flow velocity.

The reasons why this happens can be traced back to several causes, which I will not attempt to describe here, but what we do know is that the effective flow capacity depends on the amount of WIP released. So far I have always seen this happen, so I will use this assumption without trying to prove its validity; for me it is common sense.

If there is very little WIP, well below the installed capacity, the flow will also be little. This was obvious: if there is no work, there is no production.

What is not so obvious is that an excess of WIP released in the system also reduces the flow. So we can establish the following:

> ***For a system with finite capacity, the flow rate depends on the WIP, reaching its maximum flow in a controlled WIP range.***

Therefore, the second principle leads to having a mechanism to release a controlled amount of WIP, avoiding excess.

Taking into account this principle and that of aggregation, the way to program a flow is by programming the amount of WIP to be released in each period.

> **The programming of a flow consists in having a mechanism to release controlled quantities of WIP within the maximum capacity range.**

Make to Order

An on-demand manufacturing is necessary when it is very risky to produce before knowing how much and when the product will be needed.

Examples of this are special products or à la carte restaurants.

The customer always has a tolerance of time to wait for the product so the key here is to meet the deadline promised.

You are not the exception; we have all suffered the disappointment of ordering something on demand and the deadline is not met. The uncertainty grows enormously when the deadline has already been met. If the breach causes great harm to the client, the level of anxiety grows even more.

In many industries the phenomenon is known. And an improvement in on-time delivery of, say, 60% to 85% does not mean anything to the customers. Think that if there is a probability greater than 10% that they fail, you will take precautions to protect yourself from non-compliance 100% of the time. Non-compliance has a great hidden cost.

Why is it so frequent that there are breaches in so many industries? Do not manufacturers know that complying on time is one of the most valuable attributes for customers?

There are companies where they have already decided not to continue trying. I had a few years ago a conversation with the operations manager and with the production manager of a Chilean company that manufactures flexible packaging on demand. At that time they sold around USD 500 million per year, exporting to various parts of the world.

When I asked them about their delivery performance on time, they answered that it was 79.2%, considering full orders. I was impressed that they knew the number so accurately. And when I asked what they would do to improve it, they told me something even more surprising. They did not have much hope of improving it because that number was already very close to the theoretical maximum for them, who had decided that it was 85%.

That is, this company thought that the highest level of sustainable service was to offer its customers the same probability of arriving on time as of surviving Russian roulette.

How is it possible that meeting deadlines is not the usual practice in so many industries?

The reason is simple. It's because they promise deadlines based on the ability they think they have. As they allow the WIP to fluctuate much more than the controlled range we have mentioned, their delivery terms also fluctuate. And sometimes they give more than they thought and others less, so that a percentage greater than 10% or 15% of the time they fail.

And it is that nobody has told them that the effective capacity, with which they can make a good estimate of time, depends on the WIP.

On the other hand, in prestigious universities, world-class consulting firms, and other reference companies, they consider that it is necessary to reduce costs to the maximum in order to be competitive. This was one of the competitive strategies that they taught me in college.

To reduce costs, the calculation that is made is how much cost each activity absorbs in the process. To the extent that with each resource processing more units, you get lower unit cost. This is the logic.

How do we achieve the minimum unit cost? When all the resources are occupied at their maximum capacity. Wait! This contradicts the third principle of the flow: abolish local efficiencies. Is that principle wrong?

Capacity balancing

We are going to try to design a production line that maximizes the flow and minimize the cost per unit. This is achieved with a balanced line.

Although there is already a lot of literature on this subject, I will give a brief demonstration here to give support to the statements that follow.

The system we have designed has six resources, all with an average capacity of 10 units/hour. The expectation would be that the system would allow an average flow of 10 u/h.

The capacity of each of the resources is average, which means that half of the time makes 10 or more per hour, and the other half of the time makes 10 or less per hour.

The other fact that we must take into account is that it is a chain, where the last resource is able to deliver what the previous one delivers. That is, the total capacity at each instant is determined by the slowest.

For us to achieve the average flow of 10 u/h, we require that everyone is producing 10 or more units per hour at the same time. The probability that one works at that rate is 1/2. So the probability that everyone works at the same time at that rate is $(1/2)^6 = 1/64$. That is, every 64 hours, we will achieve that average in one, and less than that average in 63 hours. In a year of 365 working days, that is achieved in just six days.

I already know what you may be thinking. What we need is to achieve the independence of resources, so that the total average is that of each one. This could be achieved by flooding the plant with WIP, which generates the other harmful effect on the effective capacity that I used as a hypothesis to program: the excess of WIP reduces the capacity.

The conclusion is:

Balancing the capacities of the resources of a production line reduces the effective capacity of the line by a significant amount.

By the way, I have just shown that minimizing the unit cost achieves the opposite effect to the intended, because by reducing the actual capacity, the quantity produced is reduced for a given operating cost, maximizing the unit real cost of operating. This is why Goldratt and Ohno considered cost accounting the number one enemy of productivity.

Capacity buffer

To achieve a given flow, it is required that at least one of the resources be capable of that average capacity and the rest of the resources have an extra capacity, which we will call capacity buffer.

The magnitude of the capacity buffer depends on the variability of the process. Taking into account the large number of sources of uncertainty, this capacity buffer must exceed at least 20% of the constraint resource. That value of 20% is a minimum for very stable systems. In my experience what is healthy is to have 50% - 100% or more of excess capacity.

Also, as I already mentioned, the buffers are interchangeable: less capacity buffer leads to more time buffer, and vice versa.

Having these capacities in excess as a buffer, and knowing that we do not want to flood the production floor with WIP, we must allow the majority of resources to have waiting times to allow maximum flow.

The third principle of flow warns us against this widespread belief that leads to give work to each resource that we see idle. The phrase "I pay you to work" is wrong. The reality is that the salaries ensure availability throughout the day to allow the synchronization of the different parts, but now we see that many idle times are very productive.

> ***The fundamental error of ignoring the systemic nature is the one that leads to making decisions that block the flow in manufacturing on demand.***

The programming system in an on-demand manufacturing must comply with having the line unbalanced, controlling the WIP and avoiding measuring the individual productivity of the resources.

The TPS designed by Ohno achieved that. But as I mentioned before, Ohno said that it would have taken less than half the time to achieve everything he achieved if he had thought of the Goldratt system.

Production programming according to TOC

Programming according to TOC is to decide on what date each order should be released. Instead of programming each machine, what is programmed is each order, and once the order to production is released, each resource must work at the maximum speed it can, without errors.

Specifically, in a typical company, one will have products with longer routes than others, and experience indicates that some products take longer to finish than others.

It is important to bear in mind that in most factories, the effective processing time, i.e. the sum of all the time a transfer batch[41] is being processed, is a fraction of the total time it takes to complete the order.

Normally when I ask how much is the effective time of processing an order, what we call in TOC touch time, they tell me a much longer time than I expect.

The last time it was in a company that was delivering orders that took on average twenty days. And they told me that the touch

---

[41] Transfer batch is the amount of WIP that is usually transferred from one resource to another. If it is very large (one or two days), it is convenient to reduce it and transfer more frequently. The more frequent, the more fluid, what suits the flow.

time was four days. I asked them if we could do the route of an order and we wrote down the estimated time in each resource. When there was a debate about whether it was fifteen or thirty minutes, I put the maximum or even added them, so that there was no doubt that the calculated time was oversized. The sum gave little more than thirty hours, or less than a day and a half.

I have seen this same reasoning in LEAN literature, to show that, in this case, there is an opportunity to reduce waste equivalent to seventeen days of the total production time.

In TOC we know that the amount of time has an almost linear relationship with the WIP, so reducing the time by half, should reduce the WIP by more or less than half. And by doing this, we accelerate the flow from the first day.

The procedure is to review the average times of the production of the last months. If they vary more than 25% between some and other products, you can have two or more families. For each family, a buffer equal to half the time of those products in the past is determined.

For current orders, it is determined to which family each product belongs and the buffer is assigned. And the release date is calculated by subtracting the buffer to the promised delivery date.

This will leave several orders frozen until their release date arrives, accelerating the flow of those that are not frozen. As the days go by, the orders are released on the dates that were calculated.

> **The programming procedure is to comply with the release date calculated as the delivery date minus the production buffer.**

This action requires a lot of discipline because there will still be enough anxiety for releasing less work than several resources can do. The temptation is to "advance work" and we already know that it does not help, rather it blocks. That is, "the earlier I start, the sooner

I finish" is false in a production with a chain of dependent resources.

I will not explain here the procedure to continue promising dates with a high probability of being fulfilled, but this is what leads factories to close to 100% of delivery on time. I have a lot of experience doing it. In a Colombian steel wire factory that delivered less than half of the production on time, they reached 98% in two months. In a material factory to drill rock in Chile, 60% reached 97% in three months.

In cases that we have delayed more to reach 100% is, in part, for not complying with the release dates. The other part was not to follow the colors, which is what I will explain now.

Production control system according to TOC

The production buffers come to be a self-fulfilling prophecy. If we give ten days to each order, they will be completed in that time at the most.

But by releasing many production orders, we will inevitably have queues in front of the resources. How do we decide which sequence is the best to process each order?

What we are trying to achieve with manufacturing on demand is always to deliver on time, so the sequence must take into account the delivery date. Orders with the closest delivery date must be processed sooner.

An alternative is to be guided by the delivery date. We could have three orders, one for the 13th, another for the 14th and another for the 15th. And suppose that the first and the third require the same setup of the machine.

If we follow the sequence of dates we must make a setup for the first, another for the second, and repeat the first for the third. What do we gain with this? If it is true that the touch time is small compared to the buffer, we have wasted capacity in setups without gaining anything in compliance with deadlines.

To protect the delivery on time and allow local optimizations, the buffer is divided into three colored zones. The first third of the time turns green and is the lowest priority. The second third of the time turns yellow and has a higher priority than green. The third third turns red and is the highest priority of the orders that are on time. If the order has not been completed and its delivery date has passed, the order turns black and is the highest priority in production.

Among several orders of the same color, none has priority, allowing in our example to process the first and the third together, saving setups.

Sometimes I have seen that it is understood that green has no urgency. Let me clarify: all orders released to the plant must be processed as soon as possible; the colors dictate the sequence.

Buffer adjustments

With the system already in use it is natural to have a quantity of green, yellow and red. The stability of the system is given by an amount of red orders below 20%.

This is a snapshot every day, it is not the color with which they end. If all are finished red, we have 100% delivery on time, but in production we must have a 20% or less percentage of red orders every day.

The reason is that the rule says that color gives priority. Within the red all have the same priority. If we have many reds and several are about to fall behind, the random choice of some reds that were yellow yesterday will ensure that the other reds are black tomorrow. This is avoided if the red ones are less than 20%.

If reds are too few, less than 5%, we are releasing WIP too early. It is convenient to reduce the buffer to reduce the cycle time. The recommended reduction is between 10% and 15%. This will immediately increase the percentage of reds, keeping the system in tension for improvement.

To reduce the buffers of families, a plan for continuous improvement is required. I will not explain in detail here how to do it, I will only give a general idea.

When collecting the reasons that have led the orders to turn red, every so often you can identify what are the most frequent reasons. If projects are executed to reduce these reasons (frequent causes of reds), the percentage of reds will be reduced. These projects are the right place to use LEAN and 6-Sigma techniques.

Make to Availability

When products are standardized, in general, customers do not have time tolerance to wait for production because someone had the idea of maintaining an inventory for immediate delivery.

In this case we must ask ourselves what we seek to satisfy, because the delivery on time requires a deadline and in this case no deadlines are allowed. The good service in this case is to have enough inventory to satisfy any reasonable demand.

The word *reasonable* introduces a judgment about the necessary inventory. For example, if I manufacture screws and the model 1 x 1/2 drywall are buying me 10,000 a week and someone comes to buy 100,000, it is reasonable to think that this is a special project and it is difficult for another competitor to have so much inventory. In this case, it is also reasonable to think that the 100,000 are not required immediately and an order can be made upon request.

Inventory buffer

Clarified the special situation of an exceptional demand, let us calculate the necessary inventory to satisfy immediately any "reasonable" demand.

> **The inventory needed to have immediate availability with high probability is equal to the maximum expected consumption within the replenishment time.**

This formula is valid for all products individually.

The first thing is to understand the replenishment time. In the case of production, the replenishment time consists of the replenishment frequency and the production lead time. If the production lead time is about ten days (in the case of a production that does not have control of WIP yet, we estimate half of the current time, as we did in the case on demand), and the frequency of revision and replenishment of stock is weekly, the total replenishment time is about 17 days.

Let's see the case of a product to calculate the necessary inventory. We make a calculation with the consumptions of the last months, where we make a mobile sum for the determined replenishment time, in this example it is of the last 17 days. This will give us a sequence of sums that goes up and down. The maximum value of that sequence is the maximum consumption that was in the past in a replenishment time, and this value is what we will take as initial inventory.

That inventory value is what we call inventory buffer, or simply buffer in this context.

Start up

To start the system we must review how much inventory we have of each product compared to its buffer. If the actual inventory is smaller, we must generate production orders that complete the inventory.

If the inventory is greater than the buffer, all pending orders for that product must be voided immediately. It there is one in production, it must be decided if it is better to finish or stop it.

This first action focuses the capacity to get availability immediately and it is very likely that there is an excess of inventories, which generates an abrupt load drop in the first week.

Continuity the next day

From the next day and onwards, the inventory of each product must be reviewed and an order be generated to replenish only what has been consumed (or sold) since the last replenishment. This is done with a fixed frequency, because the time between production orders is a part of the replenishment time. If we change the replenishment time a lot, our inventory will always be incorrect: sometimes it is too much and sometimes it will be out of stock[42].

If we assume daily order frequency, a replenishment time of about 10 days, and that every day there is consumption, therefore we will have an inventory in the warehouse and another inventory in production (transit).

The quantity of inventory in production is proportional to the production lead time. And the amount of inventory available in the warehouse is proportional to the replenishment frequency. In this example we could have about 9 to 10 orders of that product in production and a quantity in the warehouse for the daily sale.

As the original calculation considered the maximum, the excess inventory on days that do not consume the maximum accumulates in the warehouse, just where we want it.

Every day orders are delivered to the warehouse and every day it is consumed, generating more orders.

Production control

Again we can have the situation of several orders in a queue in front of a resource and we must decide the sequence. Let's use the same system of colors, with the same meanings.

But in this case, the color of an order is provided by the color of the buffer in the warehouse. The calculated inventory buffer is divided into three and now green has the upper third, yellow is the third of the middle and red is the third before zero. And if it is zero, the color is black.

When there is more than one order of the same product in production, the oldest order takes the color of the buffer in the warehouse. The next oldest takes the color that the buffer would have if the first had already been delivered. And so on with all the

---

[42] Note that the popular MIN/MAX method has fixed the reorder quantity and allows time to vary, leading to this undesirable effect of incorrect inventories almost all the time. Another mystery is why it remains the method taught in so many places.

orders.

Buffer adjustment

In the case of inventory buffers, the adjustment must be made to follow the consumption trend. If the consumption is growing, the buffer must also grow, and vice versa.

The method most commonly used in TOC implementations is to determine criteria to say that the buffer is "too much red" or "too much green".

When it is too much in red there is danger of depletion and the buffer is increased in a complete zone, i.e. it is multiplied by 4/3. In this case, an order is generated immediately to complete the buffer.

When it is too much in green, we are using the capacity for an uncertain consumption, and the buffer is reduced in one zone, i.e. it is multiplied by 2/3. In this case all replenishments are stopped until it turns green again.

A warning

The only way to have inventory accumulation is having more capacity than demand.

As the production for availability presupposes the capability to accumulate inventory, in factories of this type there must always be excess capacity, it is what we call "protective capacity"

Therefore, a mechanism should be established that measures the protective capacity periodically and when this capacity buffer is less than 20%, an expansion of capacity must be executed to maintain the level of service.

> ***Only by recognizing the systemic nature of the company will the protective capacity be recognized as an asset and not as a waste.***

Project management

There are two aspects that differentiate the projects from make to order:

- The effective time of the process of a project is a significant portion of the total lead time of the project.
- Usually the tasks of a project do not obey a repetitive process, as they are in a manufacturing process.

But just as in manufacturing on demand, the important thing in projects is to deliver on time, making the full scope and within the budget.

In manufacturing, the aspect of the budget is given by the price, and the scope corresponds to achieving the minimum quality required.

The most usual in projects is that someone builds a plan for the project, in a Gantt chart, or in a PERT network, or both.

Again we see that the tendency is to want to control the activities at a very detailed level, assuming that more detail in the plan gives more control in the execution, which is false.

Planning process

Having established differences between production and projects, we know that the principles are the same but the application will be different.

We already know that the only objective of the plan is to have control in the execution. The plan is not required to give instructions on how to execute the project. If this is necessary, a separate document can be submitted to describe the tasks and the sequence, but our plan should serve to control the execution.

Again the principle of aggregation will help us reduce uncertainty to more manageable levels.

On the one hand, the tasks that we must put in our plan must group the maximum possible of activities carried out by a resource or group of resources. For example, a group of designers must produce 5 drawings, 3 calculation memories and a specification document. Instead of putting 9 tasks, we put only 1 with a duration that adds up the estimates.

Dr. Goldratt estimated that a very large project should not have more than 300 tasks in the plan.

The other source of aggregation will be to group the necessary slack that is estimated in the tasks. What we know with certainty about the duration of the tasks of the project is that we do not know them with precision. There is a low probability that a task will take very little time, and it is also low that it takes much longer than estimated. But since we are going to estimate a duration to promise a term, we need to estimate durations with slack.

For example, the previous task, with nine activities, can have an estimate of 10 days. We know that it is possible to do it in 5 days if there is no setbacks, say with a probability of 1/2 to be fulfilled so it is risky to promise it.

But if all the tasks of the project are in this situation, what we can do is take the dependent chains and estimate a time that has high probability for the entire chain. Let's take a string of 20 consecutive tasks, whose durations comfortably add up to 180 days. If we remove half of the estimate to each of the 20 tasks, we have a period of 90 days for the chain. The probability of all being delivered on time is equal to the probability of all being delayed: it is $(1/2)^{20} \sim 0$. This leads us to conclude that we need to add slack to raise the probability of delivering on time, but also it tells us that we do not need all the slack to deliver on time. Between the two extremes, with no slack or all the slack, we choose half. The slack we removed in this example was 90 days, so we will add 45 days as a buffer at the end of this chain, leaving a deadline of 135 days with a high probability of being fulfilled.

These buffers are used the same as in production. Knowing in what date we want to deliver, we subtract the buffer and it gives us the release date of the chain.

Critical Chain and Feeding Chains

In a project that already has all its tasks defined, with the estimates made, we will see two types of dependencies.

A type of dependency is when one task requires another to complete to start.

Another type of dependency occurs when two tasks can be performed in parallel but require the same resource. In this case we are assuming that the capacity is limited, which is the realistic thing to do.

The Critical Path[43] technique consists of calculating the longest chain of tasks within the project, without considering capacity limitations.

When we have capacity limitations, the shortest chain possible is the longest chain that is formed when considering both dependencies, and Goldratt called it the Critical Chain. It is not easy to determine the Critical Chain, but there are software packages that allow to do so, as long as the plan (Gantt or PERT) follows the indications given above.

Once the Critical Chain has been determined, other chains of tasks that are not in the Critical Chain, remain, but join it in different points of the project; these are called feeding chains.

The planning procedure consists in determining the Critical Chain and all the feeding chains. Their corresponding buffers are calculated as I explained above.

The buffer of the Critical Chain is the Project Buffer, and arrives at the project delivery date.

The buffers of each feeding chain reach each point of contact with the Critical Chain, and from that date to the back, the date of release of that chain of tasks is calculated.

---

[43] CPM: Critical Path Method

> ***The final program consists of the set of release dates of the first tasks of each chain, both critical and feeding.***

When the first task of any chain has been released, you must work on that chain to finish it as soon as possible.

Programming of multiple projects

A situation, which is common in engineering or construction companies, is that several projects are executed with the same pool of resources.

Actually, this is very similar to production, where several simultaneous orders go together.

In this case, the programming of each of the projects must be carried out as described in the previous section. And then, considering the point of integration, where all the projects must pass, the programming of this stage is staggered to avoid that the integrations occur all at the same time. This is the control of WIP in projects.

By doing this, the delivery and release dates will be more spread out over time, but it is the most realistic when considering limited capacity, and congestion will be avoided that would delay much more each project.

Bad multitasking

Multitasking involves doing two or more things at the same time. It is an attribute that many people value as positive, represented in the famous phrase walk and chew gum at the same time.

Multitasking can be good or bad. The bad is when one leaves a task to start another, but leaves the second without finishing it.

The good one is when the second task is finished and we return to the first one.

There are several exercises that can be done to illustrate the waste of capacity that occurs with bad multitasking. I will describe one here, which you can do in less than ten minutes right now.

On a sheet of paper you should write the complete alphabet in order, the numbers from one to twenty-six, and a sequence of twenty-six figures, repeating this sequence: circle, square, triangle and star, where you must have six equal groups and end in a square.

Put a stopwatch and measure the time it takes to do it, but you must do it in two different ways.

The first time you must jump from letters to numbers and from numbers to figures every three elements. That is, start ABC, follow 123, continue circle, square, triangle, then DEF, 456, star, circle, square, and so on until you finish. Measure the time it takes like this.

The second time write all the letters first, then all the numbers and end with all the figures.

If you are like the hundreds of people who have done this experiment under my supervision, it will take between 2 and 3 minutes at the first time, and between 1 and 2 minutes at the second time.

Note that the total of tasks is identical on both occasions, and the installed capacity, too. But we change the way of organizing work: in the first we allow more open tasks, more WIP. And only for that reason there were a series of effects that ended in waste of capacity.

In this experiment the tasks were quite simple. The greater the intellectual requirement of tasks, the greater the waste of capacity.

One of Goldratt Consulting's clients in India, an engineering company that performed well (compared to the competition), took actions to further reduce bad multitasking and the result was that after eight months they had multiplied tenfold the number of completed projects per month.

> *I do not promise any number. But do not be surprised if productivity grows more than double by avoiding bad multitasking.*

Mechanisms to avoid bad multitasking

At Goldratt Consulting we have identified four mechanisms to avoid bad multitasking. In general, they are mechanisms that can be applied to any operation, not just projects, but in projects they are essential to control the system.

I have already mentioned two: the different release dates within a project and the release dates when staggering the start of projects when there are several.

The third mechanism is called Full Kit (FK). It consists of having all the complete preparations before starting a task, and more importantly, a chain of tasks. If this is not achieved and the chain is initiated, it is frequent that it cannot continue due to lack of preparation and, in order not to waste capacity, other tasks for the resource are opened. When the unfinished preparation has been completed, the resource is now in the multitasking situation, and it is almost certain that it will be bad.

It is true that the start date of the chain may arrive and there is no FK, and it seems reasonable to start other tasks to take advantage of the capacity. My recommendation is that you do not anticipate other tasks and concentrate those resources on completing the FK. This discipline is much more effective in making good use of capacity.

The fourth mechanism is established at the lowest level of detail. Tasks can have several activities, as in the example above, with several drawings and documents. Discipline is required so that each of these activities is carried out one by one, and thus avoiding bad multitasking. In each case a different mechanism may be established, which constitutes the specific application. The important thing is that it is simple and effectively controls bad multitasking. For example, in a group of ten engineers, one must act as coordinator and order the tasks in the proper sequence. And each engineer receives only one task to work on, leaving the rest in a queue. Only when one is finished is another delivered. In cases where the tasks can have downtimes it will be better to deliver two to each engineer, at most three. My recommendation is to never deliver more than three.

Control of execution in projects

The first control is to ensure that the release dates are complied with. We already know that nothing is advanced if tasks are released prematurely.

A few years ago I worked as a control engineer in an engineering company. In one of the projects where I worked, it was the biggest engineering project that had been done in Chile, I think in history. And soon enough I saw how the meetings were very tense and the development of drawings, designs and documents had several errors. The errors were detected and corrected, but all this was wasted capacity.

In one of the meetings I attended, the project manager was present, which was not usual. Because of my position, he did not speak to me and I do not think he knew what I was doing, so, dear reader, do not imagine that I raised my voice in that meeting.

The fact is that the chief engineer of the electricity specialty told him that the drawings and documents that followed were going to be needed about six months later and, he argued, it was not necessary to start them. Most likely, other things will change later, forcing them to change. The manager told him that he did not care, that he wanted to put the project at maximum speed, so he did not want to see anyone unemployed.

> **The fundamental error, not considering the systemic nature of organizations, generates great waste of productivity by promoting a lot of bad multitasking.**

The first control is to comply with the release dates, complete the kits and avoid opening many activities for each resource.

The second thing we must control is that the project runs at a pace that allows it to be completed on time or before.

In the execution, it does not matter if the tasks finish or not on time, what matters is that the project ends on time.

For that we can use the buffers. Again we divide them into three and we put them in colors. This time the color has to do with how many days of buffer has been used compared to how much chain has been progressed. The project buffer is the main measurement.

Each time a task is completed, the days that it took is counted, and the difference with respect to the estimate is subtracted or added to the consumption of the buffer. If a task had an estimated five days and three were used, we took two days off the consumption of the buffer. If it had taken fifteen, we added ten days to the consumption of the buffer.

If consumption is still in the first third, it is green. If it exceeds but does not exceed two thirds, it is yellow. Two-thirds past is red, and late is black.

These colors allow decisions to be made regarding the allocation of resources and the activation of contingency plans.

Summary

The projects chapter is much more extensive than other operations, but the principles are the same.

The main thing is the flow of the system, for this we must control the WIP and we must have signals to make decisions. And we should not be guided by local efficiencies.

All the described programming mechanisms are designed to avoid bad multitasking. During execution, bad multitasking should be avoided with the four mechanisms described. And resource allocation decisions should be guided by colors.

There are good books and courses, as well as software and companies, that allow applying these concepts to the particular situation of each project organization: real estate, construction, engineering, software, product design, molecule development, and many more. It is much simpler than conventional methods, but very difficult to adopt, because you have to accept that many resources are not occupied in several periods.

Distribution

This explanation will be very short because I have already delivered almost everything in the production section for availability.

> **Remember that inventory is only required to satisfy a "reasonable" demand for standardized products that are expected to be available for immediate delivery.**

How many chain stores, supermarkets, pharmacies, or others do you know where one can get excellent availability? My experience indicates that few.

If you think I'm exaggerating, make a list of ten things you usually buy at the supermarket, indicating brand and format (do not accept substitutes). And now go to the supermarket to look for them. If you do this about three times, I think it's guaranteed that something will not be found in some of those visits.

Again let's use a little math. Suppose a company is considered really good because it has 95% average availability of each product. This means that your list of ten products has a 0.95^{10} probability of being complete in the supermarket on any given day. Did you calculate it? The probability is 59.87%. In three visits I would have a 20% chance of going out with everything every time.

Even that 95% availability is too high for the standard of most stores, at least in Chile.

Again we ask ourselves the uncomfortable question of why this happens. Is there anything more important for a store than having the product available when you want to buy it?

Apparently yes: the logistic cost. The theory is that if you keep the logistics cost low, you will have more profitability and you will be able to maintain good prices. Otherwise prices should go up and then sales would drop.

The logistic cost is comprised of storage cost, transport cost and even some include picking costs[44] and movements. To reduce it, economic batches are calculated: purchase, transport, picking, etc.

Each time a batch is made, the replenishment time increases.

When the replenishment time increases, the necessary inventory (or buffer) also grows.

There is something that we must keep in mind regarding the inventory: it always has errors. Either it is too little, and it runs out, or it is too much and it doesn't turn over.

Of these two errors the worst is too high. Are you surprised? Intuition can say that a stock out is worse because a sale is lost. But when the inventory does not rotate, which is the same as saying it was too high, several other things that reduce profitability occur:

- It occupies space and prevents replenishing what it does rotate.
- It also immobilizes capital, and sometimes this prevents the replenishment of products that are selling better.
- To sell it off you have to give discounts, which in itself reduces profitability.
- But in addition, discounts divert money that could have been spent on higher margin products (cannibalize profitability).
- And to liquidate it is necessary to give good space of exhibition and attention, again at the expense of the

---

[44] Picking is the operation of collecting the different products for a shipment from the positions where they are stored.

products with better margin.

> ***The fundamental error, of not recognizing the systemic nature of the supply chain, leads to excess inventory, which reduces the flow of products and cash, and reduces the profitability of the entire chain.***

Planning and control of the supply chain

At each storage point an inventory buffer must be determined for each product. We already know that this buffer depends mainly on the replenishment time.

Except in the warehouse of the plant, which must wait for production time, or in the case of a warehouse supplied by import, which must wait for the trip from a remote place, the storage points have a very small transport time, of a day to a maximum one week.

As the replenishment time in this case is transport time plus time between orders, nothing prevents to replenish daily, reducing this time to a few days.

By replenishing only what is consumed daily, the inventory will be much smaller and at the same time it will have an availability of 98%. And the stock outs will be solved very quickly.

And we use the same adjustment system that was described above, using the colors, to increase or reduce buffers in each node of the chain.

Effects of reducing batches in cost

And reducing the batches would not increase the logistics costs? Let's see.

The transportation cost would increase if we increase the number of trips. Every time I ask the retail companies, they tell me that a truck goes every day to the stores. Sometimes more. This means that today the travel cost is incurred every day, so changing the composition of the cargo will not make any difference in the cost of transporting for the company.

As for the cost of storage, reducing the batches also reduces the buffers, which reduces this cost.

And the cost of operation of the warehouses, considering picking, dispatch, etc., is normally fixed.

In summary, my experience is that the real logistics cost does not grow. But what if it grows? Would it be justified to reduce the batches?

To answer that question it is necessary to estimate the impact on sales first. The hypothesis is that before reducing batches and replenishing consumption, together with the dynamic buffer management, there are stock outs along with excess inventory. And both stock outs and surplus are reduced by switching to this mode of operation.

What impact does it have to reduce the stock outs? Usually what is out of stock is what you underestimated in your calculations, so it is quite likely that if you reduce 1% of stock outs, sales will grow 3% or more.

Being that the level of stock outs at stores exceeds 10% and sometimes more than 30%, the impact of increased sales is quite large.

Let's do a very conservative calculation to understand what I am saying. Assume sales for 100, with a gross margin of 30 and a total profit of 10. This tells us that the total cost of operation is 20. Within this cost is the logistic cost along with many other costs. Being exaggerated, suppose that the logistics cost represents 10% of the total cost (which is very exaggerated). That is, the logistics cost of this company is 2.

After applying the concepts I have described, the stock outs are reduced by 5%. We already know that sales grow at least 5%. In this case it would be an increase of 5, contributing 1.5 to the net profit. So that it is not justified, if the logistic cost grows 1.5 too, which would be an increase of 1.5 / 2 = 75%, or almost double. This is far from being probable, because for that I would have to increase personnel and trips in that proportion.

Experience shows that sales increases are much greater than 5% and that costs do not increase, rather they are reduced by reducing inventories (less capital, less space needed, fewer discounts and less waste).

Summary

The explanation of how to control the WIP, in this case is the inventory in each node, and how to control the system with colors, is simple. However, there are supply chains that require tuning the application to solve situations that I have not addressed here.

Each of the special cases requires a lot of extension and I do not want to be out of focus. I will name a few more to guide you to look in other sources if it applies to your case.

One of those cases that is not described in detail here is when the product is low rotation and the proper buffer is 1. In fact it can be that a calculation gives 0.1 units, which is impossible to keep. Then we will have 1, and when it is consumed one, we have a stock out until it is replenished. If we use the 0.1 of this example, see that we are actually saying that the probability of sale within the replenishment time is 10%.

When it is depleted, what is the probability of consuming a second unit of this same product before replenishment? It is 10% x 10% = 1%. That is, a unit gives a 99% availability. There is a whole further development to decide when to discontinue low rotation products.

This leads to the second consideration in the management of the variety. We do not want it to grow too much, so as not to fill up with inventory and, worse, confuse customers. There are already developed methods of WIP control also in terms of variety.

And finally, a very important aspect, how to handle each point of sale to improve the shopping experience. Here there are also methods developed to control the WIP and speed up the flow.

Support functions

All operations that a company must sustain to support the flow of products or services, but that do not directly generate the product or service, are support functions.

Examples of these operations are all the paperwork of purchases, sales, billing and collection. Or quality control, which does not produce, and sometimes destroys product units. Or maintenance.

The first thing we can say about these support operations is that we do not want them to be flow limitations under any circumstances.

> *Support functions must always have visible protective capacity.*

Once I talked about this topic with a friend, who at that time was a finance manager in a large company in Chile. And when I told him that support operations should always have excess capacity, he changed his face a bit and told me the following story.

In his company they have measured the level of money to be collected in amount of "street days". Those responsible for recovering money are in a collection department, with full dedication. One day he passed in front of the room where the collectors could sit to telephone and plan their routes, and he saw four bill collectors seated, where three of them were visibly relaxed at that moment.

Seeing these people idle at that time, he called the collection manager to "rationalize" the department, that is, they fired one (or two, I do not remember). Not a week passed and the number of street days increased by 20%, with a significant impact on cash flow.

My friend ended up telling me how he had to rehire to solve

it, with the consequent additional expense of the previous dismissal and the training of the new one.

> **The fundamental error, of not considering the systemic nature of companies, leads to interrupting the flow by "optimizing" support functions.**

The problem

As I already said, the first thing we must ensure is protective capacity. This immediately tells us that all the work that needs to be done must be done, and there must be time left. So it does not make much sense to schedule delivery dates or deadlines.

But on the other hand, everything I've said about the excess of WIP and bad multitasking is also true in this case.

What will be the biggest obstacle to the productivity of people working in support operations? The story that I just mentioned is a clear example of this obstacle: the fear of being fired if one seems to be redundant.

This is not typical of Chileans. In a company in Colombia they had the same problem with the technical service. In this company they sold coding equipment, such as Zebra printers or those that are put into high production lines to mark batches and expiration dates. All these equipment require service from time to time, and repairs. The technical service is a post-sale support operation, and customers expect it to be agile in solving their problems.

Each day a number of service orders appeared that had to be taken care of. It was not possible to foresee how many would arrive the following day, so that those that were pending became the visible workload of the entire department.

Now imagine that you are one of the technicians. Will you hurry to finish all the orders as soon as possible? What would happen if the company sees that there are "too many" technicians? The observed behavior was what one expects from intelligent people with experience. They made sure to always have a line of orders, so that everyone was busy.

> **The fundamental error, of not recognizing the systemic nature of the company, leads people to delay work, to look busy.**

Programming and control

Again we see that what the system wants is maximum flow. So the proposal was to design a system that achieves two things: avoid bad multitasking and make visible the necessary protective capacity.

The first is achieved by giving the head of the department all the orders to prioritize them. The sequence can change at any time if you want, but does not release them before there is capacity to do them.

Each resource (can be a technician or a team of technicians) is given between one and three orders. Never more than three. One is the ideal, but there are tasks that have downtimes, such as the installation of software, which can take twenty minutes and one must wait for it to end. In that case with two or three orders, we will make good use of the capacity. If you have three and must wait for something, you can take action to accelerate one of the three to finish as soon as possible.

When one is finished, another is given. When there are no pending orders left and there are resources that have unused capacity, it is time to account for the protective capacity.

The second thing is to make visible the protective capacity, because if there is not enough, we must build it. But before hiring anyone else, let's reveal the capacity we currently have.

How do we persuade someone to show that they have too much capacity, when that has cost someone the job in the past?

In the case of the Colombian company we did two things:

- The company made a solemn declaration to all employees that there would be no layoffs to reduce costs ever again in the future. [45]
- The technical service department is offered a bonus proportional to the sales that becomes effective only when they can demonstrate a preset minimum of protective capacity.

The bonus must be proportional to the sales so that the beneficiaries do not have an incentive for more hiring that dilute their bonus. But at the same time, they will want to earn it, so they not only work as quickly as possible and without errors, but there is also a great collaboration between them to help each other and to teach each other.

The result was that the backlog was finished within the first week. And after several months, sales doubled, doubling service orders, and the department did not need more technicians.

In each particular case, assignment methods and colors may be needed to determine the correct sequences, but the principles are the same: control the WIP, do not look for local optima and execute in the correct sequence.

Summary

One of the promises of TOC is that it must be simple. In all the solutions I have presented to manage operations of different types, the simplicity has consisted in applying four principles.

Applications can be more or less difficult to implement or design, but they are simple. And all the systems that I addressed are very complex. This shows that it is possible to build simple solutions for complex systems.

In this chapter we saw how to manage the internal system, although it was inevitable to make references to external parties, such as customers or suppliers. We will see in the next chapter how

---

[45] Later I will show the depth of this action to solve chronic problems of the economies in the countries.

to manage the relationship with customers to achieve the synchronization of the broader system, where the market is just another part.

Systemic approach including the market

In the previous chapter I focused on internal operations and how to synchronize them to achieve maximum productivity. It was inevitable to refer to some frequent needs in the market, such as meeting deadlines or the availability of products. In this chapter I want to deepen how to integrate the market in our system, how to get the company to synchronize with customers, so that everyone wins.

Blue oceans

The first idea I want to propose and develop is based on the fourth principle of TOC. This principle says "never say I know", and this means that every situation can always be substantially improved.

It is true that the saying says "the best is the enemy of the good", and in TOC we often apply it when we advise not to continue "optimizing" a solution when it is already good enough.

The principle refers rather to a radical change, which generates a level of performance that we could consider impossible if we were not seeing it.

In May of 2000 I had the opportunity to take charge of the production of a factory. If someone had come in to tell me that they knew how to increase productivity by 30%, I would have believed it but I also believed that I was capable of achieving it. If they had told me they could show me how to double productivity, I would not have believed him; Isn't it true that it sounds somewhat insulting?

I had read all the Goldratt books I had been able to get but I did not really know how to apply the concepts. Rather, I did not know anything about how to do it. Looking back I understand why; those books describe methods and techniques, and without specific details. I needed to understand what I am transmitting here. The fundamental idea is to synchronize the parts of the system so that everything flows.

The fact is that I was in charge of the production and we had a highly productive numerical control machine, which was always scheduled with large batches to process them very fast. My first action was intuitive: that machine had to work to synchronize the production rather than to demonstrate its great capacity. The order was to process components to complete parts and not many equal components to speed up the production of that machine.

The first reaction was resistance. They told me that the efficiency was going to be reduced a lot by the amount of changes that were required in that machine to achieve what I wanted; the changes would multiply by more than ten! Of course, we will make the pieces we need, but at what cost! All these were the reasons for not doing it. Since I was the manager, I asked for a few weeks of collaboration. And the changes did multiply, for more than ten.

In the first week of June, one month after this decision, the factory manager came to my office and asked me if I had already seen the productivity of the month. Honestly, I had had such a difficult month with the clients, because I was also the sales manager, I had not seen anything. He did not believe me, he thought I was teasing him. There he told me that productivity had doubled, which was the historical record of the plant. He added: "Tell me what else I should do to implement it immediately." At that time I had no more ideas in my head and I asked him to continue with that same action. In the first week of July we could see another 50% increase, that is, productivity tripled since May.

That day I decided that I would study TOC thoroughly, and that I would dedicate myself to this. Almost twenty years later I am writing this book so that many readers can absorb these concepts much faster than I did.

I would have considered insulting a promise to double productivity. I would not have even considered one tripling it. Today I know we were only at the beginning.

The year 2005 appeared a very interesting book that talks about this very thing. It is titled Blue Ocean Strategy[46] and its subtitle says "how to create unopposed market space and make competition irrelevant".

The term blue ocean comes from the metaphor they use to describe markets where competition harms each other, to the point that they are like red oceans because of the blood that is spilled in that competition.

The book describes several ideas that created such situations, such as the Cirque du Soleil, which redefined the circus show. And they also show that all those revolutionary ideas had been tried before without success, and that after several pioneers, there were some who succeeded.

It does not sound very attractive that way, where one works and fails for others to benefit. But the reality is that stagnation is not a good way either. Something has to be done to keep progressing.

By the way, there is not a big novelty in all this, right? In any basic marketing course you learn that the key is differentiation. That is the goal. How to do it is not so clear in those courses. And these professors, authors of the book, at least propose a direction.

What are blue ocean strategies based on? Goldratt

---

[46] Blue Ocean Strategy, W. Chan Kim, Renée Mauborgne, 2005

described it in other words (less poetic) when talking about the creation of a *Decisive Competitive Edge*.

> ***In TOC, a decisive competitive edge is obtained by satisfying a significant need of enough customers, in a way that nobody has achieved until that moment, that is very difficult to imitate, and that carries low risk.***

These are several demanding conditions that must occur at the same time. What I propose here as an idea is that it is always possible to achieve it, because ultimately everything is reduced to knowledge.

More knowledge leads to better solutions, also to understand why they are better decisions and to communicate them in a simple way.

I had already mentioned that knowledge is unlimited, so there is no reason for competition to take place in gaining markets in a zero-sum game; where what one wins is lost by another.

If we accept the fact that it is always possible to improve everything substantially, we will accept that it is always possible to create a blue ocean.

What about the typical sources for differentiation? Don't they create these kind of edges?

There is a source of advantage that I want to rule out at this time. Being "cost leader", which means having the lowest price. This differentiation is based on the belief that buyers always prefer a lower price.

You know from your own experience that this is not true. Just look at the computer you use or the car or cell phone. Probably not the cheapest ones you found.

And yet, there is always a pressure on the price. My explanation is that none of the competitors is making a difference that is significant.

A significant need is a limitation that customers have in their own system. Until we understand the systemic nature of the relationship with customers, we will not understand how to generate these decisive competitive edges that Goldratt talks about.

> ***The fundamental error, of not recognizing the systemic nature of the relationship with customers, prevents most companies from generating blue oceans.***

Unsatisfied significant needs

To build one of these blue ocean advantages the key is to find significant unmet needs, and be able to meet them, and that this does not mean an unacceptable risk to the company.

I already mentioned that a need always manifests itself in a limitation of the clients. If customers are business, it is a limitation that prevents them from doing their business better. If customers are consumers, the limitations are manifested in not being able to do something or spending too much time to do it.

Let's see examples of known limitations.

Most companies need to buy something on demand, in general they are raw materials. When the delivery period is not met, the production process can be stopped. In general, and knowing that this can happen, customers are forced to take expensive precautions in time and money to protect themselves from missed deadlines. This limits their ability to do a better business in turn. Suddenly we find a supplier that is able to guarantee delivery on time. It is clear that this removes a relevant limitation for our business.

Another example. We are in 1854 and we are architects. We are interested in thinking of better ways to use urban land in densifying cities. And it occurs to us to go to the Crystal Palace Exhibition in New York, where we find that a man named Elisha Graves Otis has installed an artifact that allows people to go up and down several floors with enough security, without using stairs. It is clear that this invention removes a limitation and allows us to project buildings of greater heights than those it is reasonable to build only with stairs.

In the first example, the solution offered by the supplier does not innovate in the product or reduce the price. What it does is to apply the knowledge I explained in the previous chapter and manages to remove that limitation.

In the second example, the solution is technical knowledge that solves physical limitations.

Both examples have in common that they apply knowledge to remove limitations.

Generic method to find significant needs

In this chapter I want to show the TOC method to investigate the unmet needs that could be a source of advantages.

I will rely on the first principle of TOC, which says that every complex system contains an inherent simplicity. This means that systems are composed of interdependent parts and that the more complex they are, the less freedom a part has to move without impacting another part. So we believe (from the principle) that we can always find that aspect connected to the whole system, directly or indirectly, that controls it.

It's like those domino constructions that can be knocked down with a single movement, knowing which is the piece that triggers the reaction of successive cause and effect that is knocking down the chips.

When we study a system and focus on finding the manifestations of unsatisfactory functioning, we can collect a list of facts, which we will call undesirable effects, which we know from the first principle, that are all connected by cause and effect to a root cause.

When finding the root cause, we will have found a significant need, because by eliminating, or at least mitigating, that cause, we have generated a great benefit in the system. This occurs because the root cause is a direct or indirect cause of several negative effects. By eliminating the cause, the effects are also eliminated.

The TOC specific tools to do this research are, mainly, the Thought Processes, that is, the evaporation of clouds and the logical branches. There are courses and books available to learn how to use these tools, so I will not make here an exposition of how they are used. What I will say is that not only they serve for this type of studies, but to think about any topic that interests us.

How is the cause attacked and an offer generated?

This method will lead us to discover contradictions that prevent the cause from being removed. They prevent it either because the necessary actions generate another group of more undesirable effects, or because the knowledge does not exist to eliminate the contradiction.

For example, a big problem that we observe in general trade is that you do not always find the product you are looking for in your usual store, although there is plenty in other stores. An action that could solve it is to have more inventories but, as we have already seen, the excess of inventories generates more undesirable effects than we are solving. As long as the knowledge that I mentioned in the previous chapter is not applied, the equilibrium situation will tolerate stock outs.

By the way, it's no surprise that this is such a widespread problem even though you've read the solution in this book. There are already several companies that are applying it with great success, but they are the least. The difficulty I already said: it is a cultural change.

Another example is that we are still using very expensive and polluting technologies for transportation. In this case, the knowledge to remove the limitation is in development, and when it is mature, it will be a breakthrough.

In any case, the second principle of TOC says that it is always possible to eliminate the contradiction. That we cannot do it only reveals that we do not have the knowledge to do it... yet.

In the examples I gave, the second one was a lack of technical knowledge to economically achieve something that nobody argues with: it is better to use less polluting energy.

But in the first example, the lack of knowledge of most retail companies has its origin in that they are unaware of the systemic nature of supply chains and continue to accept the apparent contradiction with techniques to reduce costs which have dominated that industry.

I have excellent news:

> *There are still many opportunities to generate blue oceans by recognizing the systemic nature of companies.*

I will give below several examples of how you can build these types of advantages without even having to innovate in product or technology yet. Then I will talk about innovations that require knowledge of science such as physics or chemistry, to name a few.

Immediate applications of systemic thinking

The following are examples of decisive competitive edges that can be developed by any company in the world if they decide to adopt systemic thinking to manage.

An advantage has always a limited life. Those who fall asleep on their laurels suffer the consequences of stagnation. These are advantages today, but in a few more years, whoever reads this book will say "that's not an advantage, it's the standard", and that's the way it should be. Each of these is a first floor of the building, to continue building.

Not all the advantages described apply to all industries, nor is it an exhaustive list. Each company must see if the conditions apply or not to their particular case or they can think of something based on the ideas presented.

The fact that the advantages described below are based on permanent needs is relevant. This means that all the changes that are made to develop this advantage should be stable procedures for the future. The constant change towards improvement does not mean destroying what is built, rather it means building the new on the solid foundations that these advantages provide.

Reliability in delivery

I've talked about this before, because it's a generalized and chronic problem. And it seems incredible that after so many years of industrial revolution it is still a problem.

Let's first describe the need.

> *When the fulfillment of the promised deadlines is notoriously bad and this breach has severe and negative consequences for the clients, the reliability in the delivery is a significant need of the clients.*

We see here the definition of the target market for which a reliability offer will be very valuable.

What does notoriously bad mean? Above I have already made a brief reflection. But let's dig a little deeper.

If you, dear reader, have a chance of something very negative happening to you, you will take every precaution to avoid those effects. If it does not happen, the better, but one is prepared all the way with some insurance, or alternatives, what we call "plan B".

These plans B have a cost, so one would like to avoid them, but they are better than suffering the consequences of the event. Would you be prepared differently if the probability of occurrence were 20% than if it were 70%?

It is ridiculous to think that one would prepare only on the occasions that occurred. If you had those divination powers you wouldn't be reading this book.

The problem is precisely that you do not know. So there is a threshold where one is willing to tolerate the problem below a certain percentage of cases. For example, I prefer one airline over another because of its punctuality. As long as my favorite is delayed very rarely, I still prefer it.

The conclusion is that reliability has a tolerance threshold, which triggers plan B when it is exceeded. It depends on the industry and the damage, the acceptable reliability in the promised delivery starts at 95%, and from there up to 98-99%. But less than this generates the need for plan B. And customers who have not planned, suffer greatly when the delay occurs.

This means that a 85% on-time delivery is just as bad as 50%. Those managers that I told you in the previous chapter did not understand this, even though, being manufacturers, they also suffer from the same in their relationship with suppliers.

There is another element that makes the requirement of reliability more demanding. When one makes a purchase of several products, the manufacturer measures the reliability of delivery by item, but the order needs all the items to be delivered. The more items an order has, the less likely it is delivered on time. If the average reliability is 90% and the typical order is five items, the probability per order is 0.95^5 = 59%. This is what they call OTIF[47].

In reliability one can distinguish the case of frequent purchases, sporadic purchases and projects.

The frequent ones are typically purchases of special raw materials, or parts with special design to be used in the production itself.

---

[47] OTIF: On Time In Full.

Sporadic purchases are usually the purchase of an equipment on demand or any special piece that is not usually required.

And in projects we have the whole range of possible projects: a house, the engineering for an industrial installation, a custom software package, and many other similar examples, where the interaction between supplier and client is frequent throughout the development of the project.

In different situations, different offers will be different. But all have in common that one promises to meet a deadline and offers a guarantee to back the promise.

Until today, and after several years, I have not come up with another way to guarantee the promise than by offering a fine for non-compliance. If you can think of a better way, I will gladly compensate this knowledge with a bottle of your choice.

> **The penalty for non-compliance is offered in an amount for each period of delay that makes sense. It is the minimum fine that one would not offer if there was not a high probability of meeting the deadline.**

For example, in the manufacture of labels, the usual terms are 10 days. A delay of one day is quite noticeable, so 10% per day is adequate. In the case of steel cables, where the terms are 45 to 60 days, 3% per day of delay is already aggressive.

In the case of projects of several months, the fines can be 2% to 10% for each week of delay, but in this case the offer may include bonuses per advance per week. In this way you can offer a minimum price for a competitive period, offer the fine guaranteeing the deadline, but asking for a reward per week in advance.

The case of projects is special because a project always has an expected return that supports the financial and time effort. And the contractor's relationship with the client occurs in the investment stage, where the focus is on cost. But each day in advance can advance the return on investment, so the offer described in the previous paragraph is appropriate. The minimum cost for a term is offered, that term is guaranteed and a participation of the anticipated return is obtained in case of getting ahead.

As I said, the amount of the fine should be the minimum that one would not offer if he had doubts about delivering on time. This is really differentiating. If competitors do not have that control that allows them to deliver on time with high certainty, then they will not match the offer. It is the same moment where they implicitly declare that they are not sure of the term they are promising.

How do we get customers to understand the value of our offer? Ha! That question has been asked to me hundreds of times. We will see how to communicate with the market later in this chapter, but this element is fundamental; if it does not communicate well, it will not persuade and all the generated value will be lost. It's what we call capitalizing on the advantage.

And how can we be sure to deliver within the promised deadlines? Look again at the previous chapter and you will find the answer. The key is to have control of the operation, and this control is obtained by controlling the WIP and governing the priorities with a simple system.

I repeat it, it's simple. But it is far from easy, otherwise, everyone would be very reliable, and they are not.

The difficulty is that most companies still do not recognize the systemic nature of their organizations, and are caught in wrong but very popular beliefs (resource efficiencies, unit costs, etc.) And those beliefs lead to the opposite of controlling the WIP. And we already saw that a WIP without control makes the effective capacity fluctuate, which in turn makes it impossible to anticipate the date of termination of an order. And this is why this advantage is very difficult to imitate.

And if one promises the fine and does not pay it almost never, it is very low risk for oneself, which is fulfilling the last requirement to call it a decisive competitive edge, as Dr. Goldratt called them.

Increased inventory turns

This subject has also been touched when I explained the production for availability. Let's go deeper to understand the customers.

> **When our customers have most of their cash trapped in inventory and availability is still an issue, improving inventory turns is a significant customer need.**

This defines the target market for the offer. They are not the consumers that go to a store, who value availability, as we will see in the following advantage. In this case, they are companies that we will call distributors.

In this context, wholesalers, retailers, and anyone who buys inventory to sell it to earn a margin is a distributor. When I say distributor will be in this broad sense.

A distributor has a business because the manufacturer does not reach all consumers. Of course there are cases of vertical integration, where the manufacturer has stores. I have helped some. But let's consider the general case where the distributor is a company other than the manufacturer.

The manufacturer is the one who can solve the significant need with an offer, but before explaining the offer, let's understand the client better.

A distributor has capital that invests in warehouses, transportation vehicles and inventory. Most of the capital is in inventory, at least the cash that remains as working capital.

The limitation that this distributor has is capital, and some also space. If you can get a little more return on the capital trapped in inventory, immediately the profitability of your business improves.

And what does the business consist of? To buy inventory and to sell it more expensive. The difference is the margin. But this is not all, the speed at which this happens is also important in profitability.

If we add up all the generated margin, it is not the same as if you get it once a week than if you get it once a month. In other words, if the inventory rotates faster, the margin generated per week grows.

Let's see all the possibilities to increase the generated margin. One is having more variety of products, because that way is to have more different channels that generate profit. But it is limited by capital, so you cannot expand the range of products if you don't have the capital to invest in that additional inventory.

Another alternative is to speed up the sale so that it rotates faster. This is done by many distributors when the inventory is about to expire or get obsolete; it's called liquidation. The discounts accelerate the sale of units, but the generated margin does not grow, many times it is less than that generated at normal speed. But time also constrains him and he must accelerate the sale of inventory that did not rotate as expected.

The last alternative is to reduce the inventory of each product without reducing availability.

This is where manufacturers show little empathy with their customers. Volume discounts and minimum purchase batches achieve the exact opposite of what we want.

Let's see the issue of discounts. If a distributor accepts a discount of 5% for buying a volume equivalent to four times what he requires before the next replenishment, in the total set of the business it seems that its profitability grew 5% in that line, but the greater volume prevented to replenish stock outs or to expand the range.

For example, you buy a product that costs 100 and sells at 140. Your margin per week would be 40. If you accept the discount, your margin would be 45, but if the constraint of capital and space prevented you from selling other products, doing the math, those additional 5 are much smaller than what you stopped earning.

Increasing inventory turns is definitely the key to increasing profitability; It is a very significant need.

> **The most attractive offer for most distributors today is one that increases their inventory turns more than twice.**

Imagine that you are a manufacturer. The normal thing for most products (except those with high turnover such as soft drinks, or short-lived products like bread), is that they buy it once a month, or every two weeks. I mean the same product. In a portfolio of 50 products that the distributor is buying, each purchase will include 10 to 15. There are several that he does not replenish because they still have inventory. If the purchase frequency is weekly, when replenishing only one third of the portfolio, the average time between replenishments is three weeks, and not one week as it seemed to be.

What would happen if you offered to that distributor that he starts buying more often only what he sells? Let's say that now he only buys what he sold every two days.

The immediate effect on the inventory that the distributor holds is that it is reduced to less than half[48]. And replenishing as often, the shortages are reduced to a minimum. Most likely, distributor sales grow a lot as shortages are eliminated. This combination guarantees an increase in the rotation of these products to more than double.

I'm being very conservative. Our customers have seen the real effect and it has always been much more than doubled. It is not uncommon to see rotations 7 to 10 times more.

---

[48] From 21 days to two days there are ten times, but the inventory is not reduced so much because now the maxima of two consecutive days are a much higher percentage over the average than in the case of aggregating 21 days. I think it can go down to a third or a quarter, which is less than half, as I very conservatively said in the text.

As for sales that grow by eliminating shortages, the effect is also greater than one believes. Here it applies what Pareto said, most of the effect is due to only a small portion of the elements of the system, the principle known as 80/20.

A few years ago I had the opportunity to talk with the vice president of logistics of a pharmaceutical laboratory in Bogotá. It is a medium-large company. I started asking him if he had shortages and he told me, with a broad smile, that he did not. Knowing that he was unlikely to apply systemic thinking, I bet on a cause. I told him that he must have a lot of inventory then, and he confirmed it. He told me that he had arrived eight months ago and had started a production policy of zero stock outs, and that in those eight months sales grew more than 40%, without discounts.

There I asked him about the initial level of shortages, waiting for a number close to 10%, and he confirmed that it was 5% at the beginning. This confirmed in that case the Pareto prediction. He was happy and satisfied with his policy.

It is natural what happened because the shortages are produced among products that were sold more than estimated, and these are the ones that actually rotated the most, independently of the estimates.

Too bad I was not there to congratulate mistakes, and trying to be delicate I made the following reflection. This year they had an extraordinary result due to the increase in sales, which was achieved by eliminating the stock outs. He nodded pleased. And surely next year the shareholders will ask for a similar result, but if there are not shortages, where will more sales come from? That changed his face. I suggested that he also offer the clients to eliminate the shortages, which would increase the sales of their clients, increasing their own. But as he believed that this was only achieved with a lot of inventory, he confessed that he had already tried without success; no client agreed to increase inventories. Fortunately, because if they did, the problem would have been much worse. So far the anecdote, which has many more details and my predictions about the inventory penalties were fulfilled shortly after. You already know what happens: excess inventory, waste of capacity, which always ends up manifesting itself in low profitability.

The question was what would happen if we offer to replenish only what it sells every two days (or every day or every week, depending on the current frequency, we offer much shorter replenishment time).

The customer's reaction will be to look at the cost that this has. First, the increased frequency of purchase would force him to do the whole study of quantities for each product more frequently. Then he would think that he would not have discounts for volume, and in addition there would be more dispatches and more invoices, and finally to receive the deliveries, which take so much time in the reception.

I guess you've already realized that all these apprehensions have their origin in not recognizing the systemic nature of their business.

All those are very easy obstacles to solve. Once that stage is over, there are the obstacles that the manufacturer has to fulfill this promise.

To dispatch so often all that customers are selling, the manufacturer requires an almost perfect availability. It is what in the industry is known as fill rate[49]. Applying what I described in the previous chapter, to produce for availability, you already have the logistical capabilities that are required to fulfill this promise.

As you can see, making the promise is easy, but it is risky if you do not have the capability to fulfill it, and for companies that do not recognize the systemic nature of their organization, building this capability is almost impossible, so this advantage is very difficult to imitate. And it is low risk because it requires less investment.

Availability

We all have this need as consumers. Going to a store and

---

[49] Fill rate is the percentage of fulfillment of the complete order. Again, this is more demanding than just looking at the availability for each product.

not finding what we need; that disappoints greatly.

And I do not mean not finding exactly a model or a color. This type of accuracy covers a lot of disappointments, but the truth is that there is another large number of occasions where we go with an idea of what we want but make the decision only in the store, when we find something that satisfies our idea.

Let's talk about the first need. That one which is very common when buying repetitive things: the brand of rice, the sauce, the shampoo, the detergent, the ink of the printer, the medicine, and many other things that should be exactly that and not another.

In this case, buying a substitute is almost as disappointing as not buying anything. And this is a hidden disappointment for the retail, because it considers that there was stock, but the truth is that we felt forced to choose what we did not want, but it is more annoying to go to other stores to look for it and we must settle for the substitute.

In any case, the products of usual consumption require permanent availability, and the shortages have the effect that I already described.

Continuous disappointments have the effect of reducing traffic to the store, and it is known that traffic and sales are closely related.

The way to ensure availability is by applying frequent replenishment and adjusting buffers.

I already explained this in the previous chapter, and we see that it is perfectly synchronized to satisfy the need for consumer availability with the distributor's need to increase inventory turns. This shows how the supply chain is a system that increases its value by increasing synchronization.

Let's talk about the second availability, those products that are not usual purchase and where we will not search a specific item.

For example, one will buy a pair of pants, and come in to see what's there. You may end up buying the same as last time, but the options are open.

The management of this type of availability has something more elaboration, because it is not only to have and always replenish the same, but it is also necessary to go refreshing the offer. And here again comes the principle of WIP control. In this case it is counterproductive to have too broad a variety. The truth is that you get very confused if you are going to buy mustard and you find a hundred types. Some people prefer not to buy anything before making a mistake. But if the offer is manageable and one can apply some criteria, they will make a selection that makes it comfortable with the purchase decision.

This dilemma of how much variety to offer is permanent in all retailers that sell short-lived products, due to fashion or obsolescence. And the way to handle it is by buying a small initial inventory and testing in stores. As it is sold, the basic logistics solution will ensure that it has not run out. Those who rotate less are retired from the offer; this does not generate shortages, because nobody expects to find it. But while it is in the offer, it is replenished as we already know.

An important issue is coherence. If you introduce a shoe model in two colors in a store, you should always replenish at least one pair of each size in each color. There is no worse disappointment than finding, after a long time searching, the model and color we want to be told that our size is not there. It is preferable to remove it from the offer and liquidate the models that are incomplete at the end of the season.

Another way to handle freshness is to rotate the collections between stores in different areas. This does not require having large inventories, because the inventories are stored in a distribution center and only taken to the store to replenish what is sold.

This reminds me of another of the anti-systemic practices I have seen. Some retailers push the inventory to the stores and ask their suppliers to send them separate replenishment per store. This way they "save" storage and picking costs. It's what they call cross docking. If, on the other hand, the replenishment was made very frequently and directly to the store, it would be good for availability but a logistical nightmare in stores to receive hundreds of shipments from suppliers. It is better to use the distribution center and take a single vehicle from the company to each store with the mixture to be replenished; and to buy from the suppliers with a reasonable frequency. The distribution center has precisely the function of aggregating demand, an effect that is lost with cross docking.

That is, once you have chosen what is going to be sold, frequent replenishment is applied while the product is still in effect.

And something that improves availability based on the previous two, is the exhibition. Also in this aspect you can think about flow and how WIP control speeds it up, but I will not elaborate on this aspect here[50].

Availability insurance

Sometimes there is a need to have something available but that represents a great investment.

For example, the miners have trucks that carry 200 or 300 tons and have a gearbox that cost USD 500,000. If the box of a truck fails, it could mean a very big loss for the company, so it is preferable to have a box available just in case.

But if it never fails and they change the truck model, that inventory becomes obsolete and at that time it is considered a great loss.

This situation is not at all frequent, but it is possible to identify a need in this type of industry.

The concept of risk has two components: the damage of the event and the probability of occurrence of the event.

---

[50] All these aspects of retail are developed in the business novel "Isn't it obvious?", E.M. Goldratt (2009).

If the damage is moderate and the probability high, the risk is real and must be managed. If the damage is very high even though the probability is low, we can still have a risk that is worth considering.

> **When the unavailability of a good means a relevant operational risk, and the availability of the good means an appreciable financial risk, the mitigation of both risks is a significant need.**

In this case, we will take into account the financial errors that are committed by not considering the systemic nature of the organizations.

Companies are systems that generate money by selling their products or services. This can be done when the whole system is synchronized to produce, that is, income is the product of the interactions of the parties.

There are costs too. The cost associated with each unit sold will be called Totally Variable Cost (TVC). The selling price minus the CTV is called Throughput in TOC. In general, the TVC is the raw material. In some cases you have to add something else, but they are the least.

The rest of the costs are necessary to operate the system and we will call these the Operating Expenses (OE). All these are not associated to each production unit, rather they can be associated to each part of the system. It can be energy that moves machines or salaries or leases, etc. Do not have the impression that the OE are always fixed.

Let's see what happens. When the manufacturer of one of these goods, such as the gearbox of a mining truck, manufactures a unit, the only real investment he made was the raw material. And in that case, the raw material of that box can cost the manufacturer USD 200,000 (or even less).

Even if the manufacturer keeps inventory of gearboxes, it is normal for the trip from the factory in, for example, Japan to the mine in Chile, to take months.

What do you do when you want to mitigate a risk? You take an insurance.

The manufacturer can offer the miner an availability insurance for an annual premium of 8% of the cash value. In this case it would be an annual premium of 8% x 500,000 = USD 40,000 in exchange for immediately dispatching a box to have available. If you use it, you are billed full, if you do not use it and return it, you pay nothing else.

For the mining company, this solves its dilemma because the additional cost of the premium is much less than the loss of throughput that it suffers if it does not have the box.

For the manufacturer, the financial business is clear, because it receives a 20% annual return on its investment while waiting for that box to be sold.

It is a mutually beneficial deal that is not considered by the manufacturer if it calculates the cost of the box with traditional cost accounting.

Pay-per-click

Today the term pay-per-click (PPC) is popular in internet services. Many services, especially advertising, are marketed in this way. One pays only for the "clicks" that the public makes on a specific link. It is assumed that there will be a conversion from click to sale and this determines the price at which this service is sold.

But before this market was developed, Goldratt identified a need in a wide range of industries that can be met if one recognizes the systemic nature of the company itself and those of the clients.

> **When a good investment is considered too risky, eliminating risk is a significant customer need.**

An investment is good if it has a good return. And it is considered risky depending on the analysis that one does.

One of the clients I assisted in Colombia has a business that distributes inkjet machines for variable coding, that is, that information printed on the product at the time of production. For example, the barcode goes on the label, because it is always the same. But the batch number and the dates of elaboration and expiration are put to each product at the time of production.

I had mentioned this company before. I will explain in more detail this business of selling printers for the production line, which we will call inkjet.

All producers of consumer goods that are sold in formal commerce require at least dates of elaboration or expiration. For this there are several alternatives. One is manually stamping the date with ink, another is using hot stamping machines, another that we are discussing, an inkjet.

You probably have seen products that have a difficult date to read because it is no longer distinguished a number or they are blurred. This is the cheapest and slowest technology. And the products that have the dates written with dots and that read well are made by an inkjet.

Inkjet machines are capable of making a few thousand per hour, and typically are found on high-speed lines. The price of one of these machines can be about USD 10,000. For a company that sells 50,000 units per month an inkjet may seem disproportionate: in less than a day or two it is capable of doing all the production, and that is why many of these small or medium-sized companies prefer cheaper technology.

Is an inkjet good for a small company? Let's see, it is true that it may be that it is used only a few hours a month, but the benefits it has are several. The coding is much better, which opens the doors of sales rooms that are demanding with this. In addition, customers have a better brand impression and can boost sales. From the operational point of view, they are so fast that they eliminate coding errors, reduce lost times and allow a lot of flexibility.

I have done the math with several examples and it always turns out that the price of the machine is paid in a few months for the benefits it produces. But...

But the small manufacturer makes two reflections.

One is that having such a sophisticated machine should increase his cost by having to take care of maintenance, someone should buy the supplies, and after a year of guarantee, the risk of paying for the head that is a very expensive spare part. His risk of operation increases.

And the other is that using it so few hours is underutilizing an asset that cost dearly.

These two reflections lead us to consider that it is risky to invest in an inkjet, but as I said, an objective analysis says that it is good in a great number of these cases.

The inkjet distributor wants to increase sales of machines but the market that buys without hesitation is that of large producers. In terms of inkjet units it is a small market compared to the potential of small producers who could benefit from an inkjet. It is a ratio of 1:100 at least.

What can we do? Convince little ones to buy because it suits them? We already know that the seller is not the most reliable counselor in the ears of a buyer. And this one perceives a risk in this investment.

The essence of the offer is that the client perceives all the benefits of the good investment without having to assume any of the risks.

The offer is we put an inkjet on a loan on your line and you pay only for what you use it. We take charge of keeping it operational: we provide the consumables (ink and solvent), we

> **do the maintenance and repair when required. And you can return it when you want no strings attached.**

Note that we are not charging a lease because the price has to do with the client's production and not with the price of the machine.

Okay, it seems very good for customers. Even when we went to see the first ones, they distrusted because it seemed too good to be true.

But how is this deal good for the distributor? It seems as if now the whole risk is assumed by the latter. Let's see if it is true and if it suits him.

The distributor must pay the manufacturer each inkjet at dealer price, which is at least 30% to 35% less than the sale price. And for this you can request a financial lease in the bank for 12 months.

Our initial calculation was that the average invoicing of the inkjet in PPC deal would cover the cost of the leasing and there would be profit. The reality showed that we fell short, and with the PPC deals the machines were paid in 8 to 10 months.

But this is not all. The promise that is made to the market is not a brand new machine. We promise you that you can mark your products with the best technology. That is, we do not sell machines, we sell the result of using the machine. This leads to those that are returned can be used in other deals.

And here we got unexpected benefits. An inkjet has a lifespan of 8 to 10 years in high production. But in PPC deals, its useful life, which depends mainly on its use, is extended several times. Still, after several years, I do not know of any termination. So after less than a year, each PPC deal produces a throughput like the sale of three to four machines.

Regarding spare parts, the distributor must also have them

available for large customers, so the investment in this item did not increase much. And the risk is reduced when one has many machines, because not all will fail, so the risk assumed by the customer was much greater than that assumed by the distributor.

It seems easy to imitate... when it is understood well. But the truth is that success is in the continuity of the service, which requires maintaining the inventories with the buffer system and managing the technical service as I explained in the previous chapter. The competitor that fails in one of these aspects will lose all his customers.

Again the mutual benefit comes from understanding the systemic nature of both the distributor and the customer.

Competitive advantages based on innovations

Although I consider innovations to all the advantages I just described, I will use the term innovation in a more restricted sense, to describe inventions. In general we can call this category new technologies.

Examples of new technologies are the elevator, the car, the telephone, the cell phone, automatic threshers, printing, new applications for mobile phones, etc.

In my opinion, the first thing to do is to apply TOC and build one of the above advantages, which gives a space of years to think about the next advantage. [51]

Assuming that we are already enjoying the highest productivity, that is, the stability and growth that derive from some of these advantages, let's think about what we can develop next.

Whatever the new technology that comes to mind, it will give us an advantage if we are able to capitalize on the benefits that technology produces.

---

[51] This is true today, but I hope that the time comes when building those capabilities does not give an advantage; it will be mandatory to operate.

Dr. Goldratt designed a process to analyze new technologies, so that it can be understood in a simple way how they produce the benefit, and then design the communication.

The process is based on the following proposition:

A new technology generates benefits if, and only if, it removes a limitation of the system.

And the process consists of four initial questions:

1. What is the power of the technology?
2. What limitations can be removed with that power?
3. What rules or operation policies are in place to deal with the limitations?
4. What new rules or operation policies would allow taking advantage of the technology?

After answering these questions, there are two more that have to do with communication to the market.

5. Considering the previous answers, what changes would improve the technology?
6. What is the best way of communicating these benefits to the potential market?

Goldratt designed this process when he studied the case of ERPs[52] and the evidence that accumulated pointing to something was not right. Many companies implemented an ERP and their results did not improve.

The example he chose to explain it was that of the MRP software packages. Before having an MRP [53], factories required several people, working several days, to calculate how much and when they should buy for each raw material needed according to the production schedule, and then plan when they would start

---
[52] ERP: Enterprise Resource Planning, is the generic term for software packages to integrate all the parts of an organization.
[53] MRP: Material Requirement Planning, software to plan procurement of materials for production.

producing each order. It was so laborious that it was done once a month.

With the first MRP, feeding the system with production orders and with the "formulas" that say the materials required by each unit, you can make the calculation and issue the procurement lists and the bill of material by order, in a lapse of 10 hours.

Many of the companies that bought an MRP saw how this task accelerated a lot, and now it took much less time to do the whole calculation... once a month!

All this is real. It does not look like it, but some of those who laugh at this story, made the same mistakes with the ERP.

Let's apply the first four questions to the MRP:

1. The power is to calculate in a few hours the needs of materials based on a predetermined formulas.
2. The limitations are having to give deadlines of more than one month, not being able to adjust production programs, having to fix the program for the entire month.
3. The current rule is to do the program once a month.
4. The new rule is to make the program more frequently, it can be every day.

Now it seems obvious, but there were many companies that did not take advantage of this technology immediately, even having bought it.

In the case of PPC that I explained above, something that accelerated a lot the analysis of whether or not it was a good investment was to realize that, for that market that perceives high risk of investment, it is always a new technology whatever it is that we are selling.

In the case of the inkjet, it is an old technology, but it is new for all those small companies that do not use it.

Sources of innovation

One of the new developments of Goldratt Consulting after the passing of Dr. Goldratt, in June 2011, is the process of innovation.

One of the important characteristics of TOC is that it develops processes to think. A process is a sequence of steps that transforms one thing into another. In general we can say that any process should take a problem and result in a solution.

The generic process of innovation has four steps:

- Improve value proposition
- Design the business model
- Design the execution plan
- Launching of the new generation of products/markets

For steps 3 and 4 we have procedures in TOC that can be consulted in other sources, and even the fourth will require communication and publicity skills that have been developed for a long time and new ones are emerging with digital technologies.

I will explain a bit on what the first and second steps are based on.

Improve value proposition

There are three sources from which ideas can arise to improve the value proposition that a company can offer:

- From the point of view of the product or service
- From the point of view of the clients
- From the point of view of the markets

From the product

A product or service can be improved with changes in its attributes. It is possible that a change in an attribute generates a relevant benefit, although no one has requested it but many would appreciate it.

I think this applies to the introduction of the iPhone; when Steve Jobs introduced it, cell phones were that, telephones. Some models were already offering incipient messaging services, and very few allowed to visit websites, but with very little practical use. But there were signs that some did want more functionality in those terminals.

When he presented it, in an epic presentation (like the ones he did brilliantly), he began by saying that he would show three products: a cell phone, a browser and a music player. How many consumers were demanding that on a single device? Few. How many people today accept that their device is only a cell phone? Still less.

These changes of attributes can even be new inventions, but at any rate, you can always examine what value is being created when using the questions of a new technology. And this is a process that allows you to discard in advance new products before investing in prototypes, which is very valuable for companies.

An example of new technology that should never have been developed in a product for sale is three-dimensional television. It is easy to say now, that failure can be proven, but we can do the same exercise, imagining the enthusiasm of the inventor, who supposed that the crowds would line up to change their devices for this superior technology.

First question, what is the power of 3D TV? See the images with volume.

Second question, what limitations can be removed when we see images with volume? Frankly, in my opinion, none. The flat images already have a sense of depth that gives the realism necessary to enjoy what one is seeing.

Third question, what rules are followed to watch shows or movies without 3D? You sit in front of the television and watch your show.

Fourth question, what new rules are required to enjoy the 3D?

You have to use some lenses that allow you to see the volume. In fact, without glasses, that 3D image appears distorted.

In summary, it does not remove any relevant limitation and also forces me to be more uncomfortable with those lenses. It was not difficult to know that it would not have any success.

Every time someone discovers or invents something new, they get very excited about the novelty, but the filter of the first four questions shortens the analysis a lot to see if it will be an improved value proposition or not.

From the clients

In this case, the analysis is very similar to what we traditionally do with TOC, investigating undesirable effects that clients suffer at present.

As I have already described, the process is to list several undesirable effects and the root cause is sought. When I explained it above, the root cause was some supplier policy, so changing that policy, and aligning the internal operation with the new policy, made a very valuable offer.

But sometimes the root cause is that the current product or service has that limitation and no one yet thought of how to improve an attribute.

An example can be that drivers sutter during the day by the sun and at night by the headlights, as well as other possible inconveniences that arise from not being able to control the tone of the windshield.

If a windshield manufacturer is able to incorporate the ability to change color and opacity of windshields, it could meet this type of requirement. Again it may be that few people demand it, but when it is available, if this power removes any real limitation, many will prefer it to the current alternative.

If you do the exercise of the four questions, you will see if there is a good chance of generating a valuable proposal or not.

And if this filter passes, then the fifth question comes, what changes have to be made to improve it even more?

Imagine that the inventor designed the system so that with a combination of codes on a keyboard he can make changes in tones. When the fifth question is asked, the design can change to replace the keyboard with sensors for the hand, where with gestures you can change the tones.

This method has several of the components of a systematic process. The technological solution requires knowledge of science, which confirms once again the statement that knowledge is what creates value.

And for this exercise, which is of invention, I suggest exploring also the TRIZ method, invented by Genrich Altshuller[54]. TRIZ is a method to invent technical solutions, but its logic is very similar to TOC. Many times I have seen that the TOC conflict cloud leads to the same reasoning as TRIZ's conflict matrix, but in TRIZ there are at least forty natural science principles that guide the solution.

From the market

Goldratt used to say that sometimes there are small signs in the market, where 1% is asking for something and companies dismiss it as irrelevant, because they are very few. And he referred to this as a "tail moving", and he said that where there is a tail moving, there is probably a dog below it; one takes the tail and captures the dog.

The method here is to detect that extreme group that tries to satisfy a need, with great effort, but that does not have an easy solution. And then invent something that meets that need at a much lower cost of effort and money.

For example, in the 1970s you could see some people who carried large radios with them to listen to music on the street. They were very few and probably considered eccentric, in addition to that more than one bothered by this attitude considered

---

[54] And suddenly the Inventor Appeared: TRIZ, the Theory of Inventive Problem Solving, Genrich Altshuller, 1996.

transgressive. For them it was a great effort to move with these great devices.

But by examining what need they are satisfying, one can think about how to satisfy it at a much lower cost and effort. In this case the market for the Walkman®, and later for the portable digital players, was immense.

The process consists of:

- Detect any of these needs that only some "crazy", 1% of the market, try to meet at a large cost and withstanding efforts and hassles.
- Understand what limitation we are trying to remove.
- Invent the product or service that reduces the cost and effort to remove that limitation, this is where we are guided by the "power" we need to create.

Design the business model

When we already have an innovation we must answer the sixth question, how to communicate the value to the market? But first we must decide what we will sell to the market and how; this is the business model.

For this decision we must take into account two fundamental things: how to capture the greatest value, and how to incur the minimum risk.

An example of a business model that I believe may have a latent risk is that of Nespresso®.

Nespresso came to satisfy a need for gourmet coffee at a much lower cost and an almost non-existent effort. Instead of having an expensive machine that makes coffee in a process of buying expensive coffee, grind, prepare, wash; the Nespresso machine does the work in one step with a capsule.

They must have thought that their business model was to sell capsules, so the machine sells relatively cheaply.

The latent risk seems to me to be that the capsules can be copied. While writing this, I did a search for "nespresso alternative capsules" and found several, among others, some coming from Germany with "Premium certification" and other products of a Chilean venture.

The business model can take several forms. In the advantages section based on systemic thinking, I showed some.

You can sell the product, or the use of the product. It can be leased too. You can sell very cheap equipment and consumables with good margin.

There are several ways to offer the same product in different ways. We must choose the model that minimizes the risk of the clients and the company, and that maximizes the benefit of the clients and the company.

The key is to offer a win-win deal, which I define as a deal of mutual benefit and mutual commitment.

Selling Decisive Competitive Edges

If we have done a good job with innovation, we can suppose that it will indeed deliver real value, and that it cannot be obtained in any other way than buying our innovation.

This leads us to a communication that must be oriented to show what limitation is removed and how our product or service is an economical and convenient way to remove it.

Many times I have seen sales techniques that are based on handling objections and achieving closures. It seems to me that this is far from generating the synchronization of the company with the market, which is the systemic approach to selling.

The three conditions for a sale

For a sale to be made, three conditions must be met: credibility, need, timing.

Credibility first in the seller. That trust that one deposits in another because it shares values and because it has a good reputation. Simon Sinek has a good theory that supports this claim. He calls it the Golden Circle[55], and he explains it in a book and talks that are found on the internet.

The credibility in our product. This, actually, is inherited from the first.

Second, the need we are satisfying defines our target market. Our communication should be clear in this regard: what will you get if you buy from us? It's interesting how people make all the connections quickly when one touches a sensitive fiber.

And finally, it must be the right time for the client. It is possible that one has confidence and needs the product, but not today. And if one receives a call offering the product, could find it unwelcome, and may even cause rejection.

The best time is when the potential customer calls asking for more information. This occurs naturally in commerce, where consumers approach the store or when buying online. In businesses where the sale is personal, the best results are obtained when someone calls you.

Therefore, the communication must be oriented to get calls. Communication that must achieve that trust, and that must convey a clear idea of the need that is satisfied.

I read something in a sales book that I thought was very sensible: "nobody likes to be sold, but everyone loves to buy".

When one is already called, the sale also has a process.

The sale process

The sale must be prepared. I mean that sale that requires personal interaction, not the one that happens in a store or online.

The aim of the salesperson's preparation, as Goldratt

---

[55] Simon Sinek: How great leaders inspire action
https://www.youtube.com/watch?v=7HvYUIH4mkA

structured it, is to overcome six Layers of Resistance.

The first thing I will say is that nobody has an innate resistance to change. And nobody has resistance to improvement. However, our experience is of heavy resistance to the changes we propose. This should lead us to conclude that, probably, we are the ones who do not know how to express the change well in order to identify the improvement. There is a good video on the internet that talks about this[56].

Assuming that the change we propose is a real improvement, let's see what layers of resistance we must overcome in order to achieve the client's collaboration:

- Agreement on the problem
- Agreement on the direction for a solution
- Agreement on the solution
- Agreement on that the solution has no negative effects
- Agreement on the possibility of overcoming all the obstacles to implement the solution
- Overcoming the un-verbalized fear

The agreement on the problem is precisely the recognition of the need. The direction of the solution has to do with what circumstances or attributes we propose to change. The solution is our concrete proposal.

After these stages are over, there are two layers that could discourage buying. On the one hand, the purchase could generate negative effects, starting with the price if it exceeds the benefit. But there may be other possible drawbacks that our product generates. And finally, buying our solution can be prevented by obstacles. If the first three layers were overcome, the buyer already has an enthusiasm to buy, and will collaborate with the supplier to overcome these last two.

And, finally, the sixth layer is not sixth in the order, as the first

---

[56] Do people resist change? https://www.youtube.com/watch?v=YvV0-_seI3I

five are. This is one that can condition the buyer to not analyze the proposal.

The first five layers are the reasons why the change may or may not be an improvement. And they are overcome with reasoning. The sixth are psychological factors that can prevent the buyer from entering into the exchange of logical reasons.

Usually the blocking of the sixth layer occurs more frequently when we have requested the interview. On the other hand, when the client called to find out more, the blocking of the sixth layer has been greatly reduced.

These layers are a guide in the seller's preparation process, where he understands how to maximize benefits, and how to minimize risks.

> **The purpose of the sales process is not to sell; is to validate, together with the client, the convenience of the deal, for both.**

The presentation should be a conversation that generates favorable emotions. All decisions are made, mainly, obeying our emotions. Did you never say I will not do it even though I know it suits me, because I do not feel comfortable? Or vice versa?

It is true that there are colder people and only listen to their reasons. If our logical preparation is well done, the sale is almost assured. For the less "cold", it is good that a sequence of emotions is generated that ends in the conclusion "this is what is convenient for me!"

Reviving the need awakens a little anxiety. The direction gives hope of being able to have a solution. The solution and solving the concerns about the possible negative consequences, gives the joy that is possible. And overcoming all obstacles ends up confirming the confidence that this is the correct change.

What is your sales experience? A conversion of less than 30% or more than 80%?

> ***Traditional sales processes often fail because, by not recognizing the systemic nature of the relationship with customers, they do not seek to validate that the deals are win-win.***

When we have successfully executed the processes described in this chapter, Goldratt Consulting customers have been surprised by the high conversion rate they began to have in their sales.

Systemic Strategies for Companies

As I said before, a system is a set of interdependent elements that has a purpose.

The purpose of the system must be something desirable by all who must interact to produce it.

The strategy must be such that it achieves the purpose. But before talking about strategies for companies, let's define the terms.

Strategies and tactics

The word strategy has taken several meanings and can confuse us. For example, sometimes you hear that such an initiative is strategic, when in fact what you want to say is that it is critical or essential. Sometimes it is said that something is not in our strategy, but it is not well understood why.

Dr. Goldratt said he searched and read several books about strategy to better understand this topic. In general, strategy is understood as something very general, long-term, to which we should aim. Sometimes it is understood as the action plan to achieve a goal.

He told the story that Einstein needed to define the time to formulate his theory of relativity. Until that moment there was no agreement of what time was. Einstein did not seek agreement, he simply defined it as that thing that is measured with a clock.

Goldratt defined the words strategy and tactics in a similar way.

> ***The strategy is the answer to the question "what for?" And the tactic is the answer to the question, "how?"***

Defined in this way, strategy-tactic pairs can be found at any level of analysis that one chooses. This definition of strategy makes it synonymous with objective.

It is interesting to make these distinctions because there are often disagreements in the tactics without even talking about the objectives. Normally the objectives are not changing and it is easy to reach agreement on them. If there is no agreement on the objective, it does not make sense to talk about how to achieve it, right?

And after there was agreement on the objective, the different tactics will be correct or incorrect depending on the validity of the premises that support them.

> ***The premises or beliefs or assumptions are what gives meaning to a tactic to achieve an objective.***

The research, the evidence, and then the knowledge, validates or invalidates assumptions. It's all about knowledge.

Conditions of a good strategy

I was saying that the purpose should be desirable for all those who interact in the system. Let's look at the particular case of companies.

In the companies, the first ones that must collaborate are the clients, wanting to buy the product or service. Without income you cannot sustain a company. Maybe collaboration is not the right word; I used it here in the sense of "buy freely and gladly", to maintain the coherence of the argument[57].

Second, the shareholders or owners of the company must want to keep the capital invested in it. If they decide to invest it in another company, they must first sell to other owners. And what is said applies to these new owners.

Third, all employees and suppliers must want to collaborate to achieve a result for which customers pay and shareholders obtain a satisfactory return.

> **The key is that the interaction must be fully voluntary, because the best result is achieved through collaboration. Collaboration is opposed to coercion.**

When any of these conditions is not met, the strategy derails the company.

There are shareholders who are forced to hold the capital for a while, and their collaboration during this time is not to achieve the purpose of the company, rather their own objective, which no longer matches that of the company.

There are customers who are forced to buy something, and will not be loyal to the brand, rather they will look for substitutes or alternatives to stop buying from that company.

And the case of employees is perhaps where this phenomenon manifests most; sometimes they work in a company forced by the circumstance of not finding a better job, and their degree of collaboration is just following instructions.

> **The necessary conditions to say that a**

---

[57] Except in the case of monopoly, or taxes, one voluntarily gives his money in exchange for the product or service.

> **strategy is good are three: it gives satisfaction to employees; it gives satisfaction to customers; and it gives satisfaction to the shareholders.**

Any strategy that does not meet these three necessary conditions is a path towards the deterioration of the company.

Rereading Taylor we find similar ideas. Let's see the first paragraphs of his only book.

> *The principal object of management should be to secure the maximum prosperity for the employer, coupled with the maximum prosperity for each employee.*
>
> *The words "maximum prosperity" are used, in their broad sense, to mean not only large dividends for the company or owner, but the development of every branch of the business to its highest state of excellence, so that the prosperity may be permanent.*
>
> *In the same way maximum prosperity for each employee means not only higher wages than are usually received by men of his class, but, of more importance still, it also means the development of each man to his state of maximum efficiency, so that he may be able to do, generally speaking, the highest grade of work for which his natural abilities fit him, and it further means giving him, when possible, this class of work to do.*
>
> *It would seem to be so self-evident that maximum prosperity for the employer, coupled with maximum prosperity for the employee, ought to be the two leading objects of management, that even to state this fact should be unnecessary. And yet there is no question that, throughout the industrial world, a large part of the organization of employers, as well as employees, is for war rather than for peace, and that perhaps the majority on either side do not believe that it is possible so to arrange their mutual relations that their interests become identical.*
>
> *The majority of these men believe that the fundamental interests of employees and employers are necessarily antagonistic. Scientific management, on the contrary, has for its very foundation the firm*

conviction that the true interests of the two are one and the same; that prosperity for the employer cannot exist through a long term of years unless it is accompanied by prosperity for the employee, and vice versa. [58]

This text is one hundred years old and I think it is still valid. This book you are reading has the same objectives as Taylor's. To my surprise, I looked for Taylor's original texts to show that the administration had started with certain wrong goals and then evolved. And I found this text that declares the same objectives that I attribute to systemic management. Moreover, that firm conviction of being able to eliminate the conflict is one of the pillars of Goldratt's philosophy.

Of course, satisfaction has degrees, so companies that compete with each other for talent, for the market and for capital, can survive for a long time if there are no competitors that raise any of these satisfaction indicators well above the rest.

But this is very sad. Seeking consolation in the mistakes of others does not exactly represent a thriving entrepreneurial spirit.

> **What I want to propose here is that the fundamental error, of not recognizing the systemic nature of the companies, generates and sustains a world full of survival conflicts, both for organizations and for individuals.**

The fundamental error: origin of chronic conflicts

I can start from any angle, because in systems everything is related. I will start by operations and how the fundamental error leads to reduce all kinds of "wasted" time.

I used the quotation marks because we already know that we need capacity buffers throughout the company to achieve

---

[58] The Principles of Scientific Management, F.W. Taylor, 1919. The first manuscript of this book was published in 1911 under the title Shop Management.

synchronization, and that these buffers are manifested in idle times, which are not waste; on the contrary, they are very productive times when they allow a better flow.

But most companies still have in their culture that fundamental belief that all employees must be occupied in something to be productive.

On the other hand, we know that markets fluctuate, demand rises and falls, and sometimes we find ourselves with more capacity than is necessary for that moment. And that's where the company's management decides to "cut fat."

Until that moment, employee satisfaction is based on having some security for their sustenance and that of their family. But, regardless of the degree of collaboration and loyalty shown, you can be fired because there is more capacity or, more specifically, managers want to reduce costs.

What is the degree of collaboration and loyalty of the rest of the employees who stay... for now? They perceive that the company is not equally loyal to them. That is the perception, and perception is what matters. And collaboration and loyalty is getting lower the longer the cycle repeats.

With that low degree of collaboration, how will customer satisfaction be? It's probably going down, too. I already said that there is a balance, where customers have no alternatives and still buy despite not being satisfied. This means that, in these circumstances, the price offered is a great differentiator.

When companies differentiate themselves by price, profitability is reduced, which reduces the satisfaction of the owners, who in turn put pressure for better profitability in the only way that is immediate: cost reduction.

And we are back to the pressure of the management to reduce "waste".

Innovation is the only sustainable strategy

In any introductory marketing course they will tell us that we have to differentiate ourselves. However, it is not something that is emphasized as the only way to sustain a company, even though we see many examples that confirm it.

The vicious circle described above is broken first by recognizing the systemic nature of the companies. This leads immediately to understand that the conditions described above are necessary for the success of the present and the future of the company.

The three conditions are necessary. I am saying this in the rigorous terms that it has a necessary condition in mathematics or in logic. To achieve the goal, the condition must be satisfied.

But I have not established the goal for the companies. Many companies have established their mission, and it is different from company to company, and from industry to industry.

However, I believe I am not wrong if I propose a generic goal for all companies.

> **The goal of any company is to increasingly and continuously generate value for all its stakeholders.**

This goal includes the present and also the future. The actions to sustain the present must be the same as the actions to build the future.

The present is sustained with actions that allow a healthy cash flow. When the company runs out of cash to pay the current expenses and to the suppliers, the company is finished.

The future is built by investing and spending whatever is necessary for the anticipated growth.

The problem is that growth is not certain, and often it is

based on weak premises. As time passes and it does not grow at the expected rate, the cash flow suffers and it is necessary to cut expenses or liquidate assets.

How can we achieve a stable present while we build the future?

As we already know, the answer to the question "how" is the tactic.

> **The generic tactic to achieve the generic goal is to build a decisive competitive edge (a blue ocean), and the capabilities to capitalize on it, in sufficiently large markets, without exhausting the company's resources or taking real risks.**

In the operations chapter I showed how embracing systemic thinking can produce innovations today in service, in a world where delivery on time is uncertain and in a world full of incorrect inventories, which do not give full satisfaction to the demand.

In the chapter that includes the market I showed several of these innovations that can be done immediately. And I also showed a systematic method to develop the following innovations that support the following competitive advantages.

The key is to focus on one at a time. When already the internal processes are solid to give that superior service, the following one can be developed. In my experience, each of these advantages opens windows of years, which really allows the development of the next.

It is always possible to do it because everything is based on more knowledge, which is unlimited. My proposal, rather that of Eli Goldratt, is to adopt the four principles that allow us to think more clearly, which necessarily leads to growth in knowledge.

Again I see a great agreement between management theorists, like Jeffrey Liker (promoter of LEAN), John Seddon

(Vanguard Method), Peter Drucker, Russell Ackoff, Peter Senge, and many others. It is not about applying models that were successful in other organizations; rather, it is about thinking, studying the system itself and making decisions that improve it in terms of the overall goal.

Perverse incentives

It is commonplace, especially among economists, to say that the important thing is to put the incentives right.

I agree. It's very important. When there are incentives, they encourage. Therefore, the first decision is whether or not to put incentives for any activity.

Typical incentives in companies are sales commissions and production bonuses. The idea of these incentives is that if you sell or produce more, you earn more: it suits the company and suits the person. Sounds logical. Is this correct?

At this moment I am challenging one of the most popular systems of remuneration in companies. But, as you will see, I am not alone.

I will start with a statement and then I will contribute logic and science to sustain it.

> **Local incentives, such as production bonuses or sales commissions, generate anti-systemic behavior, which reduces the synchronization and the value generated by the company.**

In other words, most (or all) individual incentives for local targets are perverse: they incentivize the opposite of what we intended, which was to increase the generated value.

By contrast, one might think that I am in favor of global incentives. I do not have a restrictive opinion regarding these, understood as general profit bonuses, for example. I prefer another contrary to local incentives, which is simply not to put local incentives.

But let us understand better where this conclusion comes from. I will summarize in a few lines the thoughts of several people who, not only give their recommendation, but also explain their reasons.

Eliyahu Goldratt

I heard from Dr. Goldratt several times a reflection on the motivation of people. And an incentive scheme is part of the "solution" to improve motivation.

He used to say that the basic assumption that is made to create an incentive scheme to motivate someone is that that person would not be motivated in the first place.

That is, if you observe little motivation in people, you immediately assume that the cause is in the people themselves.

As one of the principles of TOC is not to start blaming, the alternative that remains is that the cause of the demotivation is outside the person; in the system.

Dr. Goldratt said that demotivation was another symptom of the lack of harmony, whose cause is always some kind of contradiction. And he distinguished five types of contradictions in organizations, which he called Engines of Disharmony:

- Not knowing or not being clear about how my work contributes to the overall objective of the company. If this is the case, it is difficult to have a commitment and motivate me to work.
- Not knowing or not having clarity about how the work of others contributes to the overall objective of the company. In this case it is difficult for me to collaborate with others, if I do not know why I should leave what I am doing to pay attention to others.
- Conflicts. The silo mentality with sectoral objectives in conflict demotivates by the frustration they produce.
- Inertia. The fact of following rules that were created some time ago and, when changing the circumstances, are no longer necessary, demotivates when realizing that there is no sense in some of the things that they ask me to do.
- Misalignment between authority and responsibility. When a person has been delegated a responsibility but does not have the authority to make the decisions necessary to respond, it frustrates having to continually turn to a superior to do the job.

When applying TOC, contradictions are eliminated, so motivation and collaboration grow.

In the previous list, the third point refers to conflicts that continue to exist because of that mentality of optimizing one's "fiefdom". All the local incentives aim to this optimization, which is why maintaining these incentive schemes only sustains this source of demotivation.

In a recent case, with one of our clients, I had the experience of insisting for months to eliminate incentives in production, based on productivity and targets. I insisted on its elimination, knowing that the new systemic mechanism to control production was in contradiction with that scheme. Every day that we asked the workers to follow the new priority system based on colors, we put those people in conflict with each other. On the one hand, the colors ensure the correct sequence, but on the other hand, their daily bonuses benefit from a different sequence. It is obvious who won.

After eight months, and with very low results, they agreed to change the incentive system. In less than six weeks were the results in sight, with greater compliance with the delivery date and higher productivity. As always, the mistake was mine, not insisting enough for the owner to get involved more. When he did, and understood the whole scheme, he asked for the change in the bonus scheme that led to the results.

Daniel Pink

It is easy to find the book titled Drive[59] by this author, and the ten-minute video[60] is also easily found on the internet where he explains it masterfully.

The fundamental ideas of Dan Pink regarding motivation are the following:

- Money can demotivate. If you pay less than expected, that demotivates. In my opinion, this is regulated by the labor market.
- He says that if one offers an immediate reward for work done, that is effective only in very rudimentary tasks. The greater the cognitive and intellectual component of the task, the greater disconnection exists between the incentive and the result. He shows cases where incentives may even demotivate, and worse results are achieved.
- Once he has destroyed the idea that incentives would improve productivity, Dan Pink offers three motivating factors:
  - Purpose: feeling that the own work is transcendent to oneself.
  - Autonomy: feeling that one can make significant decisions.
  - Mastery: having room to improve skills.

---

[59] Drive: The Surprising Truth About What Motivates Us, Daniel Pink, 2010.
[60] https://www.youtube.com/watch?v=Razk7UiUhl8

Simon Sinek

Simon Sinek is a speaker who started with his book *Start with Why*[61], where he talks about how leaders inspire action. This is a development looking at the organization and how it relates to the environment. You can also find videos[62] on the internet.

Years later he wrote another book, *Leaders Eat Last*[63], to explain what generates the confidence and enthusiasm to collaborate in organizations.

In the first, Sinek says that it is much more inspiring to declare why things are done than simply show what is done or how it is done. Again we see the idea of purpose in this approach.

In the second there is an idea that I find very interesting: trust and collaboration cannot be imposed. When you order, at best you get obedience, but nothing guarantees that the action is done by putting the best of the person. This is obtained when you trust the leader and you want to collaborate. So trust and collaboration, which are emotions, cannot be imposed, but they are inspired.

Sinek says that a necessary condition to inspire confidence is to create a safe environment. If one generates fear and insecurity, no doubt that trust and collaboration will not flourish.

Fredy Kofman

Kofman has written some books and is also a speaker. One of his books, *The Conscious Company*[64], talks about personal values that lead to a much better performance of everyone in the company.

But he also has videos and in one of them[65] he talks directly

---

[61] Start With Why: How Great Leaders Inspire Everyone To Take Action, Simon Sinek, 2011.
[62] https://www.youtube.com/watch?v=7HvYUIH4mkA
[63] Leaders Eat Last: Why Some Teams Pull Together and Others Don't, Simon Sinek, 2014
[64] La empresa consciente: Cómo construir valor a través de valores, Fredy Kofman, 2012
[65] https://www.youtube.com/watch?v=cgJFLR2f4rY

about incentives, giving the example of a football team. Kofman says that a team is a very simple organization, with two subsystems: defense and attack.

The goal of the team is to win. And in football, you win by scoring more goals than the opponent. If we follow the logic of the incentives, offering an incentive to the defense and another to the attackers, we should improve the result.

The objective of the defense is to stop goals, so we could offer a maximum bonus for zero goals and begin to discount for each goal that the opposing team scores. Thus the defense will do its part to achieve the goal of the team.

The objective of the attack is to score goals. The bonus starts at zero and grows with each goal they score.

Kofman's insight is that in such a simple system, with two subsystems, these incentives already distort the interests of the players. It is better for the defense to lose by 0 - 1 than to win by 5 - 4. And it is better for the attack to lose 4 - 5 than to win 1 - 0.

According to Kofman this is a problem that has no solution. The only thing that can be done is to do better than competitors. I think that Goldratt, Pink and Sinek have presented well-founded ideas to be more optimistic about this issue.

In this case, Kofman poses the problem assuming that some motivating incentive is required. He himself realizes that there are no individual incentive schemes that improve motivation. And, he says, he studied the problem for more than ten years. In the face of the evidence, what remains is, or abandon (apparently he did), or revise deeper assumptions. I already mentioned what Goldratt said: the causes of demotivation do not reside in the individual himself, therefore it does not make sense to try to solve the problem at the individual level: the fundamental cause is not recognizing the system, or not understanding how to synchronize it better.

But again, what is clear is that Fredy Kofman has laid out a strong argument to show that local incentives are perverse.

Summary

What encourages a person is something that brings him closer to his personal goal. I believe I am not mistaken in establishing that the generic goal of any human being is the same: happiness.

This goal has many different expressions, so I use this word in the generic sense that means greater personal fulfillment for each one.

About happiness there are some developments that serve as a basis to better understand how motivation works. I'm going to refer to two here.

The Nobel laureate for economics in 2002 is the psychologist Dr. Daniel Kahneman. His life's work is about how people make decisions. One of his researches was in the United States to detect how income affects the perception of happiness. The evidence led him to affirm that the perception of happiness grew as the income grew, but to a limit, after that limit, other factors influenced the perception of happiness of the people.

On the other hand, Dr. Goldratt's daughter, Dr. Efrat Goldratt-Ashlag, established two necessary conditions to be happy: to have a sense of security and to have a sense of satisfaction. These are necessary conditions, and both build a good foundation.

When observing what Kahneman discovered we see that it is totally coherent with the two necessary conditions. Most people derive their sense of security, in part, from their income, because that provides them with food and shelter. There are more aspects of security that have no relation to income, but that does not mean that they are not relevant.

Once a certain level of security has been overcome, the perception of happiness comes from other things, presumably they are things that give satisfaction. In general, the sense of satisfaction comes from reaching goals that seemed difficult: to play an instrument, to learn a language, to obtain a degree, to improve the lives of people, etc. We already see that the higher the goals, the greater the happiness they derive.

Based on these studies, it can be affirmed that money can motivate to the point of providing more security, but it is not a source of satisfaction. And I dare say that, from personal experience, satisfaction motivates more than money.

The question I have tried to answer in this chapter is whether perhaps the very popular incentive schemes for productivity (or sales commissions) drive or not the overall productivity of companies.

I had more authors to continue showing different facets of the same subject. But as everyone agrees that local incentives hurt the organization, I found these enough. You can keep looking for more references. If you find someone who offers an argument, and its corresponding evidence, to defend local incentives, such as productivity bonuses or sales commissions, I am willing to pay for that knowledge with a bottle of your choice (do not forget the evidence if you want to collect the bottle).

The fundamental idea of this book is that systems thinking creates much more value than management by silos, because value is created by interactions, where local performance is necessary up to a limit, but over that limit can block the flow through the construction of work in process, which, we know, reduces the flow velocity.

The conclusion about the incentives is clear:

> **Incentives are, in general, perverse for the system because, by not recognizing the systemic nature of the companies, they break the synchronization.**

It remains to answer how to motivate people to get their best contribution. And the answer starts with what Goldratt already told us: people are internally motivated, it is system conflicts that demotivate.

In Goldratt's ideas we see directly how to achieve better synchronization. Pink and Sinek's approaches are very coincidental, where safety and human values are emphasized, emotions that enthuse.

Theory of Constraints is focus: do what you must and do not do what is not necessary.

About what to do to achieve the best job of your employees, I can suggest some ideas here:

- Eliminate all bonus schemes for individual productivity and adjust salaries to a market payment or a little higher.
- Never lay off someone because he is redundant. We already know that buffers are necessary to maintain the flow. And sometimes the demand is reduced and it seems good business to lay off people. However, the productivity of those who remain is much lower as their confidence decreases. In this regard, Goldratt said that loyalty is a two-way street. It is the task of managers to use their capability to generate differentiations that resolve this issue. It can be expressed explicitly as a statement and practiced creatively in extreme cases[66].
- Provide a purpose to each person in the organization, showing that their work has a clearly aligned objective with that of the company. In TOC we have a tool to do this: the Strategies and Tactics Tree. With this same tool you can also show each one what is the purpose of the work of the rest.
- Use TOC to eliminate systemic conflicts. Every time we guide management teams in this task, people are grateful and it is notorious how motivation grows throughout the company.

---

[66] https://www.barrywehmiller.com: This is a US company They lost 30% of their sales in the crisis of 2008. They decided not to fire anyone, but they needed to reduce spending. They offered extra vacations without payment for four weeks, interchangeable with each other. Those who could afford more, exchanged it with those who did not want to reduce their salary. They managed to reduce the target twice and nobody was fired for excess capacity. The story is told by Simon Sinek in: https://www.youtube.com/watch?v=ImyZMtPVodo.

I can think of some other actions or suggestions, but you can see that everything comes down to improving synchronization by eliminating contradictions. And it's not different with people.

That is why training in TOC tools, especially the so-called Thinking Processes, in my opinion, generates a superior managerial ability, by facilitating the practice of systemic thinking.

Popular myths in management

In my practice of years analyzing companies and helping management teams to adopt systemic thinking, I have been collecting popular as well as false beliefs in business administration. Several of them have been exposed in other chapters, but I found it interesting to make an explicit list, which can be used as a test to examine the degree to which one does not recognize the systemic nature of companies.

This is not a totally original idea; many years ago Dr. Russell Ackoff wrote the f-Laws[67] of the administration. It can be found on the internet, but they are different from these myths.

Daniel Kahneman, the psychologist who was Nobel Prize in Economics 2002, says in his book *Thinking, fast and slow*[68], that our mind always seeks a shortcut, that reasoning is effortful. He also says that there are many illusions that try to deceive our logic, and often successfully. You have seen more than one optical illusion. When one already knows the trick he is not fooled, but the eyes keep

---
[67] "Truths about organizations that we would like to deny or ignore - guidelines for the daily behavior of simple and more reliable managers than the complex truths proposed by scientists, economists and philosophers" R. Ackoff.
[68] Thinking, Fast and Slow, Daniel Kahneman, 2012.

seeing the illusion. The fact of knowing does not change the perception.

> *All the beliefs that I describe here are like those illusions; one can understand why they are false, but they are still "trying to deceive us".*

It is a relatively extensive list and I divided it with the same logic with which today most of the companies are divided: in areas of responsibility.

Operations

Myth 1: An idle resource is always a waste

This is the first and deepest of the myths, which has led to the worst errors in management. It is a source of other false beliefs too, and I already mentioned it when I introduced the fundamental error, which is to ignore the systemic nature of organizations.

It consists in believing that the maximum productivity of the company is achieved when each of the parts is being used to its maximum capacity.

It can also be expressed as "a resource must be busy to be productive".

But that characteristic of the organizations that Peter Senge calls interdependence, or what Russell Ackoff called interactions, is that organizations are systems, and because they are systems, this belief is false in that case.

Some of the typical mistakes that are made for believing in this myth are:

- Balancing resource capacities in a productive flow. This only leads to reducing the total capacity of the system.
- Laying off personnel when they look redundant. It has

been known by better names like "rationalization", but this leads to three disastrous consequences: the aforementioned capacity balancing effect is achieved; the behavior is encouraged to fill the time to be busy, reducing even more the capacity; and it harms the perception of security that, as Sinek said (see previous chapter), is a condition to inspire confidence and collaboration, achieving the opposite of what was sought.
- Increase batches in all types of operations. Production batches to reduce preparation times; transportation batches to reduce freight cost; purchase batches to reduce purchase costs. Each time a batch is increased, the time we are programming in advance increases. The error is to try to predict exactly what we already know is uncertain, exhausting the reserves of the organization to react to uncertainty.
- Utilizing capacity today, even if there is no immediate demand, only to reduce the average cost, leads to the construction of inventories that drain the cash.

Myth 2: The earlier I start, the sooner I finish

It seems that this is obvious, but most of the time it is false. In most cases, to finish before you have to start later. This is because the capacity is limited. If I try to do two or more tasks simultaneously, what we call in TOC bad multitasking, the total speed of execution can be reduced between 30% and 90%. That is, if I do not waste my ability with bad multitasking, I could do between 50% and ten times more work with the same capacity.

You might believe that I exaggerate with the ten times, but this was the improvement that one of our clients in India observed. It is a Swedish engineering company, and the division of India, which serves the Indian Navy in the maintenance of submarines, achieved exactly this: in about nine months it was improving to achieve ten times more finished projects per month, with no more personnel.

If you want to experience it first-hand I suggest you do this exercise:

- Get a sheet of paper and a chronometer.

- On the sheet of paper you must write three columns: the letters from A to Z, next to the numbers from 1 to 26, and next to it a sequence of four figures (square, circle, triangle, star).
- Do it twice as fast as you can and measure the time.
- The first time do it changing the column every three movements, that is, write three letters, then three numbers and three figures, and return with three letters, and so on until you finish.
- The second time do all the letters first, then all the numbers and then all the figures.

Note that the second time I am asking for numbers and figures to be postponed. See what result you get. When did you deliver the figures before? When it started before or when it started later?

This myth leads many companies to waste a lot of their capacity. I remember a dramatic case in an engineering company where I worked in the area of project control. The project manager asked that everyone start all the tasks as soon as possible, because this way they took full advantage of the capacity and managed to deliver before. I could see the disastrous consequences in costs, deadlines and errors of that policy, which were evident months later, even with publicity in the press.

Myth 3: The unit cost measures the real cost

Charles Thomas Horngren[69] must be the most known author in cost accounting. I used one of his books at the university to study this subject. I did a search and found the fifteenth edition of *Cost Accounting: A Managerial Emphasis*[70], where I read in the preface the following:

> *This book focuses on how cost accounting helps managers make better decisions.*

---

[69] C.T. Horngren, October 28, 1926 - October 23, 2011, was an accounting academic at Stanford University, with post degrees at Harvard and Chicago, author of several cost accounting books.

[70] Cost Accounting, A Managerial Emphasis (2015), C.T. Horngren, S.M. Datar, M.V. Rajan.

I am going to refer to an exercise that Goldratt presented in another book[71] and that he repeated live hundreds of times. I have also presented it hundreds of times and I have used it in online[72] courses. I reproduce it in the annex as I presented it in my first book.

The exercise is designed to present a case that refutes the theory of cost accounting as a reliable means of making operational decisions.

The book that I mentioned before, that of Horngren, has almost a thousand pages, it has many editions and the authors are representatives of the most prestigious of the world academy. As I said, I used it and I believed it at the time, because a student does not question what they teach him, especially if it comes with such an aura of authority.

And then I learned about this exercise, which shows that cost accounting is not reliable as a guide for making operational decisions.

It is a shock of such magnitude that it produces one of two effects: the one who believes the Goldratt demonstration loses almost all the respect he felt for the academy; and the one who does not believe him, and seeks refuge in academic sophistication, loses his opportunity to open his eyes to a simpler and more effective alternative to manage companies. This reminded me of Morpheus offering the blue or red pill[73].

Years later I understood that the clash occurred in the same university, without me noticing! In fact, in parallel to the course where you learn cost accounting and decision-making exercises are done, there are other courses, where you learn mathematical optimization.

As I mentioned, mathematical optimization considers systems as a whole, so it is not surprising that its results are correct.

---

[71] The Haystack Syndrome, 1990, E.M. Goldratt
[72] https://www.udemy.com/course/276684/
[73] The Matrix, movie, 1999

In summary: if one tries to reduce the unit cost to a minimum, it will only achieve the maximum real cost and, as a by-product, it can even block the operation.

The explanation is simple. Knowing that buffers are required within the operation, many of its parts do not need to be busy all the time. Employing them in what is not needed consumes money and accumulates work in process reducing synchronization. Since synchronization is the key to generating value in any system, any reduction in value also reduces the value created, even to the point of creating less than what is spent in creating it.

Myth 4: Improving the layout improves productivity

Maybe it's not the most popular but I've found companies that spend time and money improving the layout.

The phrase "improve the layout" must be defined: it is the change of disposition to reduce travel times or to reduce movements in an operation.

As we already know, most of the productive processes have enough uncertainty to require large amounts of buffers, which translates into inventory in process. The normal thing will be to find that the time a piece spends waiting for something inside the system is more than ten times the time it is actually processed.

And the other fact is that most resources have excess capacity, which we know is a necessary buffer of capacity.

Both facts lead us to understand that changing the layout to reduce some time of transport or movement, will not improve productivity at all most of the time. There are cases where it makes sense, but they are the least. Many times a lot of effort is invested and almost nothing is gained.

There is a particular case that does bring great benefits and, paradoxically, it is in the opposite sense to that which is done in most of these projects.

I refer to the case where I recommend uncoupling a

continuous process.

The clearest example of this is the production of big size products, such as cars. Most of these factories are arranged to have a continuous flow in the plant. This means that one can see how all the products move together: the body goes to paint, then subsystems are assembled, such as brakes, suspension, transmission, electrical; then the seats and interiors are put in, the engine, the doors, and the car takes shape.

When a productive system is thus coupled, its production speed is equal to that of the slowest resource at each moment. But wasn't it the constrained resource which determines the speed of the whole? That is true if that constrained resource can be producing all the time: thus the average speed of that resource is reached throughout the system.

But all resources have some moment where they produce less than the constraint. Each time this happens, the entire system produces at that rate.

In an assembly line of fifty, one hundred or more resources, what is the probability that none is slower than the constraint? Almost null.

The solution is to find the resource constraining the line and separate it from the rest, allowing there to be a physical space before and after, where it is possible to accumulate pieces, so that it should not stop because any other resource of the line has slowed down.

On most assembly lines this requires a large investment to make the space, and it may be necessary to adapt cranes or material movement systems. That is, in this case we are modifying the layout in the opposite direction: adding times and movements.

The result of doing this[74] is to raise the speed of production to

---

[74] The only case that I know of was referred to me by Goldratt himself, when they did something like that in General Motors and the capacity was increased by approximately 30%.

the average of the constraint. With a 10% increase, 10% more sales have been achieved, which pays for the investment made in a few weeks.

In general, layout changes reduce space buffers and reduce flexibility to the system, reducing synchronization.

Myth 5: Reducing setup times always brings benefits

This is a specific variant of the same previous idea. When the time of preparation that is reduced is in a non-constrained resource, the speed of production of the system has improved nothing, and has cost time and money, reason why, in general it is harmful.

This is an activity that brings benefits when guided by a systemic improvement program, i.e. when a shorter preparation time increases productivity, which is usually in the constraint.

Myth 6: The more detailed the control, the more control is achieved

Some common sense is that we need a program to be able to control the operation. This is valid in a production and also in a project.

The general tendency is to detail the program to a point that allows us to later control the execution.

What is not recognized is that when I am forced to reschedule, at that moment I have lost control. Let's see what forces to reprogram.

We already know that in reality there is a lot of variability and uncertainty. From the point of view of the program, the uncertainty is manifested in that we do not know exactly how long a particular process will take.

For example, we have to program ten orders that take about two hours each. And we work eight hours a day, so we know that the ten orders will take approximately two and a half days.

The meaning of variability is that those two hours on average per order can be 90 minutes in one and 150 minutes in another. If we want to make a program that gives us control, we could make a list with the ten orders and put an exact time for each, to know at what time each order should be processed.

When six hours have passed, we expect to find order four starting. It is very likely that we will find order three still in execution, or that the four already ran for a while.

If we add to this that the next machine also has a list with hours, coinciding with the end times of the previous one, and so on with several machines in sequence, it is almost impossible that this program can be followed for more than half a day. It is time to reprogram, that is, to recognize that we have lost control.

The evidence shows that the more detailed the program, the less control we have.

The solution is the one I already described in the operations chapter. Schedule the orders and not the resources. Program by order groups at what time the first process starts and from there allow to work as quickly as possible. Since we have released orders with time buffers, the control is simply to decide on what sequence are processed in each resource based on the color code.

This program never changes and allows much better control, because it controls the performance of the whole and not of each part separately. Rather, it allows controlling the synchronization, intervening where it is required to maintain it, and, better yet, not interrupting the flow when intervention is not required.

That is, we have achieved more control with less detail in the program.

A slightly more sophisticated version is applied in projects, but the principles are the same.

Marketing

Myth 1: It is possible to build a sustainable advantage based on cost

This myth should already be buried by the experience of all of us, but as it was taught for years as part of the possible strategies (being a cost leader), I will address it here briefly.

First, what determines the value of a product or service is the combination of three things: price, quality and associated service.

The quality is simply to meet the requirements that the consumer is demanding.

The service has to do with the delivery, which can be a promised future date or immediate delivery.

The price is the lowest that complies with those two previous conditions.

For example, if I want to buy a pliers for my house, as I do not use tools frequently, it is very possible that the quality suitable to my need is low: frankly I do not care if it breaks in use number twenty-five, something unacceptable for a professional use. Therefore, I am not willing to pay higher quality.

But if I work with pliers, the cheapest one does not work for me.

I can also do the same reflection with the service. If I know a brand of pliers that meets my needs for quality and price but I cannot find it easily, maybe I'll pay a little more for the one I could find.

Quality and service are, by far, the most relevant nonlinear factors when choosing. And the prices of the equivalent alternatives are always very close to each other.

Having an "advantage" in price means eroding margins to the point of having to sacrifice quality or service. And this is not competitive, that's why I used quotation marks.

When a new technology reduces production costs significantly, it makes sense to lower the price and gain market, while competitors imitate the improvement. In this case, rather than a leader in cost, one would be a leader in innovation.

I always tell our customers not to give discounts (as long as the price is already aligned with the market), rather let us build a real advantage, based on a service of greater real value.

Myth 2: The external environment is constantly changing

I have heard many times "the only constant is the change". Witty phrase, applied to marketing would lead to continuously changing the offer, which requires a lot of effort. But is it true?

Let's think about the needs that we have already examined. For example, reliability is a need that will never cease to be relevant. And if we build an offer based on satisfying it, it is not necessary to continually change the offer.

The significant needs of which I spoke in another chapter are constant elements. Therefore, since such important elements are constant, the external environment is not constantly changing in the essential.

Myth 3: The more positive differences, the more competitive the offer

I have had this conversation with managers a few times. We have seen that a need that is very significant in their market is not being met and we execute changes in the operation to satisfy it. Now we can build what we can properly call a competitive advantage.

Building the advantage is not an easy task, as you have already seen in the chapter where I explain several alternatives.

But selling it is the real challenge.

In companies they are not used to having a competitive advantage that distinguishes them from the rest. And many times the market does not expect it either. After all, it is many years without offering what we now want to offer as a novelty.

Designing the offer, and communication, and communicating without falling into distractors, is hard. Sometimes they find it so difficult that they tell me that something else is needed to make it even more attractive.

If we already have a competitive advantage based on a concept (reliability, greater rotation, lower risk, etc.), well presented should be sufficient. If it were not, it is not true that the need was so significant.

Do not misunderstand me: I prefer everything positive ... but if it does not distract me from the essentials.

It is so difficult to build, capitalize and sustain an advantage, that temptation is big to look for other differentiators. And the problem with this is that any distractor can, and almost certainly will, endanger the whole advantage.

If we have done the job well: we identify a significant need, we build the capability to satisfy it at a much higher level, we design the offer well, we design communication well, and we work in the prospecting and presentation to the relevant target market. If we have done all this, it is not true that another positive attribute makes our offer more attractive than what we need to grow.

Sales

Myth 1: The purpose of the sales process is to sell

This is a slightly tricky phrase. Obviously more sales come from a good sales process.

What is false, in my opinion, is that a sales call is successful if the prospect has bought something that did not suit him.

I prefer to say that the purpose of the sales process is that they buy from us. Also, as I read once, none of us like to be sold, but we love to buy.

The sales process consists of presenting the offer in a way that the prospect is enthusiastic about the benefit that will be obtained by buying. And for this to be effective, the benefit must be true and strong.

Myth 2: Persuasion is an art with which one is born

From what I said in the previous myth, I think that charismatic and attractive personality, with which some are born, and that is the stereotype of the good seller, is not a necessary condition to sell well.

Persuasion is greatly facilitated if one really sells something that generates a great real benefit. And for presenting that kind of offers it is possible to train the majority of people. I have done it, with few exceptions. A good salesman is made.

Myth 3: Salesmen must be good negotiators

Again we see that the idea is to handle objections or negotiate conditions as attributes of a good salesman.

When the offer is really good, and is well presented, it is not necessary to negotiate, because there will always be more buyers than we need to fill the capacity of a period. And we do not need to win everything. Negotiating means reducing the benefits for the company, and this is bad management if the capacity remains full with sales under normal conditions.

Myth 4: Commissions correctly incentivize salesmen

This was a point already addressed when exposing about motivation.

When would I pay commissions for sales? When the salesman decides what, to whom, when and how he will offer products. That is, when the salesman acts as an independent agent. And he can be an employee of the company, but he behaves as if he were an independent agent. This is how the following two paragraphs should be understood.

The problem with this scheme is that an independent agent has clear conflicts of interest with the company in terms of the conditions he will offer to customers. It is convenient for the agent to reduce the margin to increase the volume, and that discount never subtracts only the commission. It also suits him to offer all kinds of guarantees and shorter terms.

But the worst thing is that the agents compete with each other for the clients. Teamwork is a phrase that is used a lot, precisely because it is missing.

However, if the sales force is an integral part of the company, with a clear function in the commercial value chain[75], a fixed compensation is the most appropriate[76].

Myth 5: The greater the magnitude of the change, the greater the resistance

To demonstrate the falsity of this claim, Goldratt conducted an experiment in public. He said first that he would choose a volunteer at random and propose a huge change. So big that it would change his relationship with all his acquaintances. Family, friends, work, etc. And we will measure the time it takes to accept or reject the proposal.

We choose someone and we offer him the winning number of a lottery that pays USD 100 million. And before he accepts so quickly, we make him notice the consequences in his life of receiving this award. And they always accepted it in less than a second.

---

[75] Justin Roff-Marsh is an Australian expert on TOC who has developed the idea of reengineering the sales function, using the concept of division of labor. Some design the offer and the communication, others do prospection, others schedule appointments, others execute appointments and a Customer Service assists specific orders and solves problems.

[76] A market salary or a little more, and a stimulating environment, where you feel the security of working in a solid company that creates real value, is motivating enough.

It is not change that produces resistance. It is the uncertainty that comes with the change. No one resists improvement, and every improvement is a change. But we all have enough experience to know that few changes are real improvements.

Myth 6: It is logical that greater volume has greater discount

Cheaper by the dozen is a commonplace.

When it comes to deciding if one accepts an especially large order, there are certain considerations to make in deciding the price.

What is a very large order? Let's say that I produce and sell things that have a normal term of twenty days of delivery. If someone wants to buy from me a volume equivalent to forty days of production, that's large. Given this volume, many managers study a lower price to win the proposal.

Accepting the proposal means that for forty days I will be paying the costs of producing to produce the volume of that order.

And this assures me that I have forty days of spending already covered, which produces tranquility... for a few weeks.

It also means that the rest of the clients should be postponed for more than twice the usual term. And that could jeopardize future sales.

As you know, I start from the assumption that it is always possible to have a competitive advantage. If I have it, the normal thing will be that I never miss the orders. If I have between ten and fifteen days of committed load, my term of twenty days will be reliable and sustainable.

If I accept the order with a discount, for forty days I have reduced the gross margin in the same proportion, while the expenses remain the same. This erodes that month's profit by three to five times the discount, or more. And if you also jeopardize the service to other customers, it is very possible that you only agree to accept that request for an increase in the price.

When you recognize your constraints, you understand what determines the profitability of the business. When the capacity is limited, it is not advisable to give a volume discount.

Distribution

Myth 1: Larger inventory is required to offer better availability

I already explained in another chapter how the necessary inventory is determined to offer availability. And the most relevant factor was the replenishment time.

The greater the time of replenishment, the greater the inventory. But if the replenishment time is reduced, the inventory is also reduced.

That belief assumes that one cannot do anything with the time of replenishment. And we already saw that much can be done to reduce it.

The belief is false.

Myth 2: The closer the inventory is to the consumer, the better

This belief is based on a reality. If there is no availability, there is no sale.

However, if one keeps most of the inventory in a distribution center, and only replenishes what is consumed in stores daily, availability is better and the total inventory in the chain is lower.

So the opposite is right. It is better to keep most of the inventory farther away from the consumer, where the uncertainty is less.

Myth 3: Replenishing small batches reduces logistics efficiency

This can be true if one measures the logistic efficiency as the cost of the logistic function per unit of product moved.

But if we measure the cost for each product sold, we can have a surprise.

With all the explanations already given, it is clear that large batches increase the replenishment time, inventories and inventory errors. These errors are surplus of many products and shortage of some others.

Excess prevents more products from moving, faster.

Shortages reduce sales.

If we reduce the batches in all the links of the supply chain, we will reduce the inventory, its errors, speeding up the flow and increasing sales.

We can end up moving fewer units, selling more and at a lower logistic cost per unit sold.

Finally, many times I've been told that you cannot send a box in a truck; It is anti-economic. So I ask how many times a truck goes to the store, and it's once a day most of the time.

If a full truck goes once a day, and in the store does not accumulate infinite inventory, it means that the equivalent of one truck a day is sold. Please, now send the truck with few units of many products: those that were sold the previous day.

Ah, but the picking will multiply! ... Well, I do not want to scare anyone, but if you have to work, I hope you work.

Strategy

Myth 1: It is necessary to know the internal strengths before setting the course

You will recognize in this phrase the technique known as SWOT[77], and you will also have seen that the emphasis of this book is on creating the conditions that one wants to generate stability, growth and sustainability.

The first thing is to decide what market need we are going to satisfy. And then we will decide what internal capabilities we need. If we do not have them, we build them.

So far we have never required to rely on an internal strength to build what was required to compete. This is a very static analysis, which presupposes that the company cannot build what it lacks of.

The course is fixed looking outwards, not inwards.

Myth 2: The competition is a zero-sum game

Fortunately, this belief is less and less accepted, but there are still managers who make decisions as if they believed it to be true.

It would be zero-sum if there were no more value to create, if there were to be distributed what there is.

As I believe that knowledge creates value (not automatically), and knowledge is unlimited, then I believe otherwise.

And the evidence of the last two thousand years shows it.

Myth 3: It is important to be aware of the opportunities to take advantage of them all

This belief is similar to the one I mentioned about marketing, where another positive attribute could improve the attractiveness of the offer.

In this case we believe that any opportunity that presents

---

[77] SWOT: strengths, opportunities, weaknesses, threats.

itself will not do so again, so we must take advantage of it while it is within our reach. For example, a large order that covers our capacity for forty days.

Most of the time, opportunities divert attention and de-focus us. When we lose focus, the organization loses synchronization.

If we keep the focus on our competitive advantage, the right opportunities will find us prepared to take advantage of them.

Myth 4: There are many independent factors that determine a strategy

The greater the complexity, the fewer the relevant constraints, because everything is interconnected. An element cannot be affected without affecting many other parts of the system.

Since constraints determine the level of performance, there are very few independent factors that determine the strategy.

And it is always to build a competitive advantage and all the capabilities to capitalize and sustain it over time. And to repeat this process adding another and another, as the processes are standardized in the company.

Finance

Myth 1: Greater profitability implies greater risk

A competitive advantage is based on making an offer that has three characteristics: it satisfies a significant need in a very superior way; It is very difficult to imitate; and it does not require incurring high risks.

The example I have used repeatedly is to offer reliability. If one is able to deliver on the date almost always is already satisfying the need. But if you offer a high fine (for example, 3% daily), it is very difficult to imitate if you do not know how to achieve it. And if you almost always succeed, the fine is not a very high risk.

On the other hand, a competitive advantage increases the

profitability of the company above the market average.

Thus we have managed to increase profitability and reduce risk at the same time.

Myth 2: With a more detailed budget, total spending is reduced

This is a particular case of the myth of control. The more detail, the more control, remember?

In this case, we ask each area to estimate how much they will spend next year. After the estimate, we reduce it, because we know that it has safety slack.

This phenomenon is repeated for so many levels the estimate is requested. And all will offer comfortable estimates, because they do not want to be in the situation of not being able to operate to the maximum due to lack of budget.

However, we also know that the estimates are forecasts, and contain the same errors as in the case of inventories: excess or shortage.

In general, most estimates have more than what was really required, and some are below, because there were surprises.

On the other hand, if one does not spend the approved budget, it is very likely that it will be cut the following year, so that most areas end up "fulfilling" the budget, although they would not have needed it.

It seems that with the last sentence I reveal my distrust for the vast majority of people. It is not like this. I trust they have experience and they know how to manage their resources. Maybe if I tell you that many of them would have worked just as well with 10% or 20% less, it better represents what I mean.

Therefore, the more detailed the budget of the company, the greater the total expense.

There are alternatives to this widespread practice, and so expensive in time and money. But we must abandon the illusion of control.

Eliminating contradictions

The key to productivity in systems is synchronization. Greater synchronization generates more productivity.

Productivity is defined as the amount of value created per unit of effort. In particular, in companies the value created is measured in throughput[78] and the effort in inventory and operating expenses.

Any increase in synchronization will be reflected in higher productivity. The concept is simple.

We can detect what diminishes synchronization in a system through the symptoms of lack of synchronization. A symptom is always something visible that bothers us because it is evident that it blocks more value or because it increases efforts.

In a system, the symptoms are always facts that bother us in some way. In this regard we have a very good intuition, because we know what we want, even if we make mistakes in terms of the means to achieve it. We will see that this last element is precisely

---

[78] Throughput: corresponds to income from sales minus what the necessary raw material cost. The most specific definition was included in a previous chapter; I'm only interested in the concept here.

where the exit of the labyrinth is.

> **I will call undesirable facts to these facts that are evidence of lack of synchronization.**

Examples of undesirable facts are: we have shortages in stores, we have excess inventory, we delay deliveries frequently, and other observable facts that are evidence that something is not right.

The origin of undesirable facts

These facts that bother us are still there because we have not been able to eliminate them. We have tried with some action. And that action mitigated or eliminated the fact, but it generated other facts of equal or worse negative charge, which forces us to take the opposite action.

That is, despite our best will, we cannot eliminate the fact until the contradiction between the actions is eliminated.

> **The origin of an undesirable fact is always a contradiction.**

Now the relevant question we can ask ourselves is: are there contradictions impossible to eliminate?

To answer us we must make a distinction between objectives and actions.

If the contradiction is in the objectives, it is likely that it cannot be eliminated, but in that case there is no system either[79].

If the contradiction is between two actions, it is always possible to eliminate it. This is one of the principles or axioms on which Dr. Goldratt founded his philosophy, the Theory of Restrictions.

Once I had the personal experience of living in the flesh this

---

[79] A system has a single primary objective. If two of its secondary objectives, what we call pre-requisites or necessary conditions, were contradictory, that annihilates the primary objective. This is easily provable.

belief of Eli (as we called him his friends). I was the director of a project with a manufacturing company, and for eight months we had had product delivery over 98% on time and, at the same time, there were about 30% of orders in red. As I knew, with more than 20% in red, the system is unstable and, with the TOC system, that produces more delays than 2%.

We traveled to Israel with the company managers to review the project, where Dr. Goldratt could assist several companies in a single week. And I met with him to inform him of the status of the project.

I was very happy with 98% but I was intrigued by 30% of reds. For months I looked for the cause and finally I started to believe that, in this particular case, 30% was stable... Eli's gaze told me more than his comments about my lack of rigor: if I know that 30% is unstable, and I have 98% delivery on time, there is something I do not know. The undesirable fact is the instability, but hiding behind the good result did not provoke a good reaction in Eli.

We had a meeting with the managers and in an hour the mystery was solved. Eli did not accept the contradiction and asked what they were doing to achieve the delivery in time of the orders that were about to be delayed.

There they said something that they had never told me. Every day they met at 7 am to choose the orders that would be processed in a workplace that was the constraint. They changed the programming, did not strictly follow the color system, and resolved the delays with much more effort.

Eli made it clear to me that this was the only case he had seen in thirty years, but that did not excuse me from having done the analysis well from the beginning. If I had not settled for the good result, having all the data in front of me, I would have deduced in a few days what was happening. After that meeting, we modified the color system to take that case into account and the company eliminated the 7 am meeting and the reprogramming. Production was increased by 10% immediately and the additional effort expended to deal with the contradiction was reduced.

The contradiction was as follows: either we follow the color system (and fall behind), or we do not follow it in certain cases. The knowledge of a very particular condition of that company (which I have not seen again), led to modify the color system for that circumstance. The contradiction was eliminated: now the modified system is followed and there are no delays, and the red orders fell to the 15% -20% expected.

In the years after that experience I had several other opportunities to observe inconsistencies and that lesson helped me maintain the discipline of continuing to think until I eliminated the contradictions. It was always possible.

It is impossible to prove that all contradictions can be eliminated. It is the belief that it is possible to do it that pushes to seek knowledge to eliminate them.

Isaac Newton had already written about this in his magnum opus[80], in Book III - System of the World, he establishes what he believes are the fundamental rules for reasoning in philosophy (or science). One of them says that nature is essentially simple and harmonious with itself. This means that we will not find contradictions in nature. And if our observation is that there is a contradiction, it is a lack of knowledge. This is how scientists progress in knowledge by observing nature.

Genrich Altshuller developed a system to invent methodically called TRIZ by its acronym in Russian. TRIZ is the inventive theory of problem solving, and is explained in a readily available book[81]. At the end of the third chapter he says:

The inventor must find and remove technical contradictions.[82]

As you can see, there is a great coincidence among scientists about this principle.

---

[80] Philosophiae Naturalis Principia Mathematica, Isaac Newton, 1687.
[81] An Suddenly the Inventor Appeared, Genrich Altshuller, 1994.
[82] Ibíd., cap. 3.

> **Contradictions can and should be eliminated with knowledge.**

The compromises no longer have a place if one accepts this principle. The compromises only preserve the contradiction, the conflict.

Current education, and even at the social and political level, has as one of its values the ability to reach agreements.

My problem is that the agreements are based on compromises. If one accepts what I have written here, agreements can never be based on compromises; agreements arise from a better understanding and advancing in knowledge, eliminating contradictions, not accepting them.

It makes no sense for someone to agree with another that the boiling point of water is 95°C. One says it is 90°C and the other says 100°C. Both have measured it with thermometers. Is it reasonable to say that it is 95°C? First we verify that the thermometers are well calibrated, or we use only one of them. And then we verify that the conditions are the same. If one of them measures it at sea level and the other in Santiago (700 meters higher), it is very possible that both have measured well, but now we understand something about nature. The boiling temperature depends on the pressure. This knowledge makes the apparent contradiction disappear. The compromise would have left both in the dark. Now the two know more.

When we are talking about organizations, composed of human beings, the knowledge of the natural sciences is not enough.

Types of knowledge

In the example of the boiling temperature there is a knowledge of how nature behaves. That behavior cannot be altered by the human being. We can say that this is the first type of knowledge, that of the laws that govern nature.

There is a second type of knowledge, which is made up of

laws that govern a part of nature: human beings. The particularity of these laws is that they exist but human beings can disobey them. And even positive laws can be enacted that contradict them, even if the laws do not change.

An example of these laws is what in economics is known as the law of *supply and demand*[83]. When one ignores this law, and fixes a price different from that resulting from equilibrium, either some consumers are dissatisfied, or some producers are dissatisfied. An arbitrarily fixed price is a compromise that leans towards one of the sides. It does not solve the contradiction and preserves the conflict, generating not only one, but many undesirable facts.

Some may argue that the equilibrium price is not reached in cases of monopoly, or if there is not enough information. I agree. That does not invalidate the law, what it does is to introduce elements that demand more knowledge.

There is a third type of knowledge that concerns the human being, that having relation with the second type, is distinguished from it in the scope of application.

The knowledge of the second type is external to each person; things happen independently of the intention of each one.

The third type could be typified by philosophy as teleological, that is, knowledge about the human being in terms of its ultimate purpose. We can identify with this type of knowledge ethics, that knowledge of good and bad in the sense that man is perfected or becomes less human.

Personally I believe that there is an objective, totally rational knowledge that can be called ethics, and that tells us which is the best behavior, that is, what behavior will make me happier, because happiness is based on better performing the ultimate goal.

It is in this field where the greatest amount of compromise in

---

[83] This law says that the price of a product or service is adjusted depending on how much the supply is and how much the demand. At the same offer, higher demand increases the price and vice versa.

social life is observed. And therefore, what a surprise!, we already know the origin of the abundant evidence that we observe around us that makes us exclaim that the world is very damaged. The undesirable facts abound. In the Jewish religion there is this goal of repairing the world (tikun olam[84]), and Dr. Goldratt said that the world is so damaged that it cannot be very difficult to improve it, even a little.

Is it possible to eliminate the contradictions that arise when ignoring the two types of knowledge that concern directly and only human beings? Ignoring knowledge does not eliminate contradictions, but I believe that it is possible to reach certain levels of agreement in basic matters that allow peaceful coexistence.

Basic distinction between objectives and actions

I have already made this distinction before to explain at what level it is not possible to eliminate the contradictions.

Now I want to go deeper into the distinction as a means to build a systematic method of eliminating contradictions[85].

I will use contingent examples to illustrate the method. When we are discussing about pensions, some say that the state should guarantee a minimum amount to retire, and others defend the system of individual savings.

In the first proposal, the actions all end in a tax, or an imposition.

In the second proposal, the actions end all in which the work performance, the foresight and individual discipline, determine the amount of the pension.

And all the discussions (at least in Chile) focus on these two

---

[84] Tikun olam, Hebrew terms that mean "repair the world".

[85] For those who know about Theory of Constraints, they will immediately recognize the tool known as Cloud Evaporation in Conflict. In this chapter I have dared to propose a mechanism more in line with the intuition of the whole world, because I have seen how the cloud makes it very difficult to learn for the majority.

extremes. And the proposals are all compromises, or at least leave implicit the assumptions of each one. And the objectives are rarely stated.

Objectives: a necessary agreement to advance

If you ask the group that proposes the guaranteed state pension, what for are you pursuing that option? The answer will declare the objective you have in mind. Suppose they say that their goal is to force the rich to pay, so that they share the suffering of the poor, even a little. I do not know about you, but I do not agree with that goal.

Note that if I do not agree with the objective, I can never reach agreement on an action to achieve it.

An alternative answer to the same question is so that no one in Chile is in such a state of indigence that he has nowhere to live, what to eat and what to wear. And this goal could be general at any time in your life, but we are answering for the period from retirement age.

Do you have any problem with this goal? I do not. Remember that the country is a system. What happens in one part has ramifications in the performance of the whole.

Now we ask the one who thinks that only individual savings should generate the retirement pension, why is he pursuing that option?

If the answer is that he wants to be well, no matter what happens to the rest, we will also have problems with that goal, because we already know that the system suffers if any part does.

The alternative answer that I do accept is to ensure that my pension depends more on my personal effort than on others.

If we have not reached agreement on the objectives, it is clear that it does not make any sense to try to reach an agreement on the means to reach them.

But once this step is over, we now have reference points for the conversation about the means.

A prior verification of the legitimacy of the objectives is that both are necessary conditions for a higher objective, which we have in common.

In this case, both conditions are necessary to have a peaceful society and provide more and more satisfactions. At least more satisfactions than those obtained from living in isolation. Before creating so many interactions, men lived much more isolated than now, where most of the time must be devoted to providing food and protection. This is a point made by Matt Ridley[86], where he shows how societies of human beings evolved by using ideas created before, unlike animals, that knowledge cannot be transmitted and, therefore, their interactions are much more limited.

That is, it is necessary to live in society to benefit from all the advantages of interactions. And at the same time, it is necessary to be a peaceful coexistence. Will there be someone who does not agree with these objectives?

Validation of premises

When objectives have been agreed, the conversation is within boundaries. It is already an advance.

Now we can examine the proposals of each one. We are in this conversation because there is no agreement on the actions, so we have to examine each one. And what I have said is that it is always possible to eliminate the contradiction between actions.

To understand each proposal we need to know the assumptions or premises that each one has considered to propose a specific action.

In the example of boiling water, both parties may have had the false assumption that boiling depends only on temperature. And as we advance in knowledge, by learning that it also depends on

---

[86] The Rational Optimist, How Prosperity Evolves, Matt Ridley, 2010

the pressure, the disagreement disappears.

If we are able to know the premises, we can validate or invalidate each of them, or understand under what circumstances they are or not valid.

An example is the typical contradiction of the inventory. More inventory to protect sales, less inventory to control costs. And the assumption that is invalidated is that the replenishment time cannot change. The actions are aimed at reducing the replenishment time and the contradiction disappears: enough inventory is kept to protect sales, and it is an investment within the company's cash and space capabilities.

The question to reveal assumptions is: why the action will achieve the objective?

In this case we can ask, why do you think it is necessary to guarantee a minimum pension to ensure that the retired people have enough food, shelter and clothing?

Here come answers, which are the premises that we must validate. And in this exercise is where the knowledge of the second and third type becomes relevant.

I will give some examples of possible answers to this question:

- There are people who had many job gaps and could not save enough.
- It is necessary to ensure a dignified retirement.

I am using these as examples of analysis, and I do not intend in this book to have a dialogue with myself so that all of you agree. This reminds me of the joke (it's a joke!) of the woman who tells her husband "whenever I want your opinion, I'll give it to you".

The first assumption is true under certain circumstances and may be invalidated under other circumstances. If the country has sustained growth, and companies are increasing their productivity, a consequence could be full employment. If so, it is invalidated from the outside. What if the person had his gaps voluntarily? This already comes to have another type of valuation, because in justice, if one did not want to save, why would it be right to give something at the expense of others?

The second assumption requires more definition, because "decent retirement" involves a judgment, where someone qualifies retirement. Is it a retirement that allows you to pay for cruises every six months and live with luxuries? Or is it one that allows you to have three meals a day and a room to sleep? Who defines it?

Maybe we can change that phrase to one that encloses something more objective, such as: "It is necessary to ensure a retirement to maintain at least the standard of living that people had while working." This is already much more objective, and it is still open to debate.

When words like "justice" are used, they have to be well defined. Justice is giving each one what corresponds to him. And it's not giving them all the same.

What is interesting in having these dialogues is that one can better understand the positive part of the opposing proposal when also understands the objective well, as long as it is a legitimate objective.

Returning to the example, a systemic vision of society should lead us to recognize that our achievements have depended on interaction with the rest. In particular, Bill Gates would never have been enriched if millions had not bought his products. And an employee would not have had a job if the customers had not chosen the company's products. And none of us would enjoy iPods if Apple had not invented them.

Therefore, it can be argued that, in justice, everyone should receive adequate compensation for their contribution, and we should all contribute to that compensation. And that's remuneration.

On the other hand, for the same reason that the value we receive is due to the interactions, none of us is benefitted when there are people or groups at the level of indigence. All these people are able to contribute with better interaction if they have a minimum level of security. How do we do it? Forcing others to provide it?

Coercing is a path that leads to minimums that are not personal achievements, which is very frustrating, and it is always insufficient. It seems that the best way is to achieve better synchronization between what people can do and society demands, organizing freely as they wish: in companies, or as freelancers, or other schemes. I already mentioned Alfredo Barriga and his book *Futuro-Presente*, where he shows very disruptive technologies in the labor relationships of the future. As possibilities grow, new knowledge is introduced that can dissolve contradictions.

What is a necessary condition for this exercise to have some result is that all those involved accept that logic is what guides correct reasoning. And logic has very precise rules, as Aristotle already established:

- A is A. Something is what it is and it is not something else.
- Something cannot be and not be at the same time.
- There is no third possibility; It is or it is not.

Leibnitz added a fourth: everything has a cause [87].

And another condition is that people have the self-discipline to change their habits when they learn something. And that's demanding.

Designing actions

Once agreed upon some premises, we can design actions that achieve both objectives simultaneously.

In this exercise it is good to anticipate all the possible negative effects that may arise from the proposed actions, and thus avoid them.

---

[87] Aristotle used this argument to reason that there cannot be endless causes, so it is logical that there is an non caused cause or unmoved mover.

It is an exercise of logic and intuition. The effects that we are going to avoid do not exist yet, before the actions are executed. We can rely on the intuition of people and, not least, their tendency to criticize ideas from others, so we propose the actions we have thought and ask for their opinion.

It is very rare that there is not at least one warning. Our job will be to turn those warnings that something can go wrong in potential undesirable facts. If you cannot write a criticism in terms of a fact, then it is an unfounded fear.

When we have made the list of potential undesirable facts, we can go one by one explicitly extracting the premises that would explain them.

Why doing this action will we have this potential undesirable fact? And the list of reasons are the premises.

Again, each of the premises can be validated or invalidated. It may be that the premise was not valid and knowledge was required, such as "the earlier I start, the sooner I finish"; or that one can add something to the action that invalidates it.

In TOC we have a fantastic tool to do this methodically. It is called the Logical Branch of Sufficient Cause.

Summary

All the contradictions that generate undesirable facts can be eliminated.

Eliminating contradictions increases system synchronization, which increases the value for all members of the system.

It is always knowledge what dissolves the apparent contradiction.

For this mechanism to be effective, people need to have intellectual honesty and a reasonable handling of logical reasoning.

Theory of Constraints, the creation of Dr. Goldratt, is the best body of knowledge to identify and eliminate contradictions in systems.

Summary of Systemic Management with the Goldratt Theory

The first movement of Academia and managers must be recognition of the systemic nature of companies and organizations in general.

I think I have provided enough logic to conclude that organizations are systems. And I also think that I will not find much opposition to this idea.

This recognition leads to study the characteristics and behavior of the systems. In this regard, my deduction, after studying some authors and observing the evidence in my professional practice, is that the fundamental characteristic of the systems is that the value they generate is directly proportional to the degree of synchronization between their related parts.

And I believe it because they generate value through the interactions between the different parts, not as a sum of actions but as an emergent result of the interactions.

> **Therefore, the key to managing organizations is to make decisions that increase synchronization.**

Synchronization increases each time a contradiction that has generated undesirable events is eliminated. And the recognition of the fact and the deduction of their cause is a fundamental part of the training that any person with managerial responsibilities should receive.

On the other hand, Dr. Goldratt's Theory is a body of knowledge with principles, tools and applications, which focuses precisely on eliminating contradictions.

So I think that, for now, the Goldratt Theory is the best body of knowledge to guide the decisions of the managers of any organization.

All knowledge about reality, whether from basic sciences such as physics, chemistry or biology, or from sciences that involve human behaviors such as psychology, economics, finance, and others, finds its place in management when it contributes to increase synchronization.

In my opinion, this is a much simpler proposal to approach management than what I have observed in the pre and post-graduate programs.

More simple, but not easy at all. The road that remains to be traveled is as vast as the knowledge that remains to be discovered.

~~~~~~~~~~~~~~~~~~~~~~~~~~

ANNEX: DECISION-MAKING EXERCISE

The operation consists of four identical resources, which spend $ 1,000 a week each, whether or not they produce (wages, maintenance, etc.). These resources work 8 hours a day from Monday to Friday, so their installed capacity is 60x8x5 = 2400 minutes/week. There are no setup times, to make it easier.

In addition, another $ 2,000 a week is spent on leases and other expenses. We will keep the example simple, so we will assume that it is a totally fixed expense.

Weekly expense:
Resources: $ 4.000
Others: $ 2.000
TOTAL: $ 6.000 / wk

Resource A	Resource B
$ 1.000/wk	$ 1.000/wk
2400 min	2400 min

Resource C	Resource D
$ 1.000/wk	$ 1.000/wk
2400 min	2400 min

And this operation, which is under your care, produces two products only:

Products	Price $/Unit	Demand Units/Week
P	$ 90	100
Q	$ 100	50

And it produces them from a purchased part and three raw materials, of identical cost per unit.

The flow of the process is as shown in the figure:

The figure is interpreted in this way: A RM1 raw material unit is taken and processed for 15 minutes in resource A. After that, it is processed for 10 minutes in resource C.

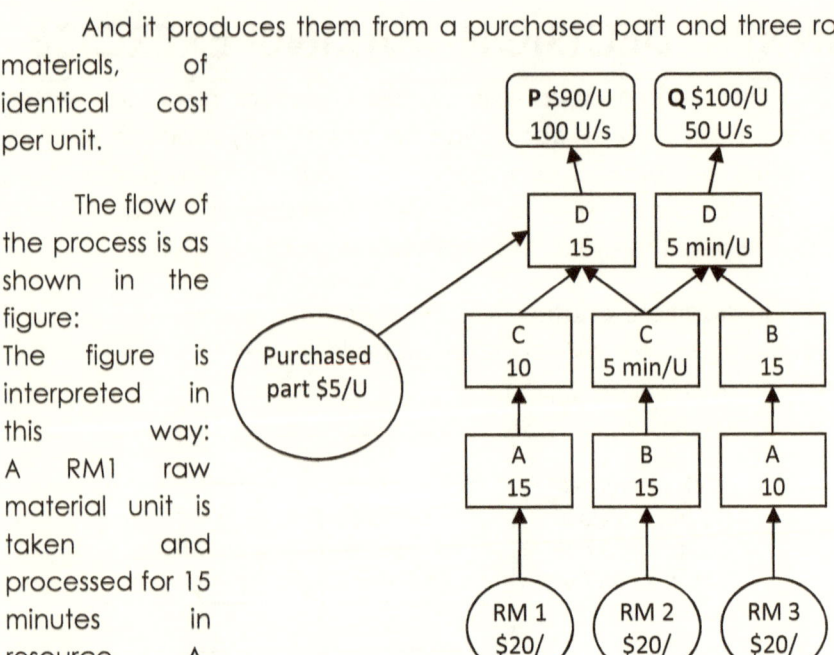

In parallel, a raw material unit RM2 is processed 15 minutes in resource B and 5 minutes in resource C.

These two parts are assembled in resource D, together with an externally purchased part, which takes 15 minutes, leaving one unit of finished product P.

You as manager of this operation want to maximize the net profit and your first calculation is to produce everything the market wants to buy:

Weekly sales	100 units of P at $ 90	$ 9.000
	50 units of Q at $ 100	$ 5.000
Raw material expense	100 units of P at $ 45	($ 4.500)
	50 units of Q at $ 40	($ 2.000)
Fixed weekly expense		($ 6.000)
Weekly Net Profit		**$ 1.500**

If you do not plan production, you may have an unpleasant surprise at the end of the week.

Let's see how many minutes we need in each resource to satisfy this demand:

Resources	100 units of P	50 units of Q	Total time
A	1500	500	2000
B	1500	1500	3000
C	1500	250	1750
D	1500	250	1750

We are asking from resource B more than it can give. It is very possible that you realize this late and leave unmet demand.

The first thing I want you to notice is that if this problem of insufficient capacity had not existed, you would not have needed to take any operational decision. Therefore, any effort to gather information would have been a waste of time. It is better to spend that time selling more, for example.

But the capacity is not enough and cannot increase it, so you have to decide the mix of products that will produce maximum net profit.

Intuitively we know that this problem is solved by finding the product that provides the higher margin, the most profitable. Let's do the exercise of gathering the product cost information first:

	Product P	Product Q
Price	$ 90	$ 100
Raw material unit cost	$ 45	$ 40
Minutes to produce a unit	60 min	50 min

Product Q has a better price, lower cost of raw material, and less production effort (which means less cost assigned by any cost accounting system, including ABC).

According to this information, the Q product is the most

profitable for the company, so the mix would be:

P	60
Q	50

Next, you receive the report of a newly hired industrial engineer, who likes mathematical models and shows you the following:

The objective function that we must maximize is composed by adding the contribution of each unit of P sold, plus each unit of Q sold, discounting the fixed costs of the operation.

The contribution of each unit of P is its price minus what we pay for the raw material and the purchased part: $ 90 - $ 40 - $ 5 = $ 45.

The same goes for the contribution of Q: $ 60.

And this function would have a maximum of infinity if it were not constrained by two things: the market and the internal capacity. With this information the following model has been built:

Max: $45 P + 60 Q - 6000$

Subject to:

$P \leq 100$
$Q \leq 50$ } Demand constraints

A: $15 P + 10 Q \leq 2400$
B: $15 P + 30 Q \leq 2400$
C: $15 P + 5 Q \leq 2400$
D: $15 P + 5 Q \leq 2400$ } Capacity constraints

After verifying that everything is correct, a computer is used and resolved. This model is simple and can be done with the Ms-Excel solver.

The result obtained is the optimal mix according to the model:

P	100
Q	30

I hope that at this point you do not despise the models of young engineers without giving them an opportunity, because what is very clear is that one of the two is wrong. Of course, costs are much simpler, so let's hope that these equations are not so correct.

Let's review the result of applying one or the other model calculating the profit that results from each of the proposed mixtures:

Profit according to cost accounting mix:

Sales	60 P x $ 90	$ 5.400
	50 Q x $ 100	$ 5.000
Raw material	60 P x $ 45	($ 2.700)
	50 Q x $ 40	($ 2.000)
Fixed expenses		($ 6.000)
Weekly Net Profit		**($ 300)**

This is bad news, but we still need to know if with the other mix more or less money is lost.

Profit according to mathematical programming:

Sales	100 P x $ 90	$ 9.000
	30 Q x $ 100	$ 3.000
Raw material	100 P x $ 45	($ 4.500)
	30 Q x $ 40	($ 1.200)
Fixed expense		($ 6.000)
Weekly Net Profit		**$ 300**

The same, but positive! So now you earn money instead of losing it.

The bottom line is that if we just found a case where the cost accounting information leads to a terrible decision, then we can never trust it again.

So now we should start using mathematical programming in all operations? That would be monstrous. At least I found it very difficult to solve this simple problem. Can you imagine what it would be like if you have tens, hundreds, thousands of products? And what about the demand, based on forecasts without any accuracy? And of the times of production, where a sick worker is enough and everything changes? To continue imagining that scenario is a nightmare, so let's think a little more.

Let's use what we already know. If there were no market or capacity constraints, the profit would be infinite. So what determines the maximum profit are the constraints.

Let's take a deeper look. Did all the constraints in the example work the same? In the market, the case of Q did not constrain the profit at all; you could sell up to 50 units and we were at 30. In fact, if all the market had acted, that is unambiguous symptom that the internal capacity is not constrained.

What happened to the capacity ones? To know, let's see again the table we built to know if everything could be produced or not:

Resources	100 units of P	50 units of Q	Total time
A	1500	500	2000
B	1500	1500	3000
C	1500	250	1750
D	1500	250	1750

Here we see that we have more capacity in resources A, C and D. So the constraint that limits the generation of profits is resource B.

Knowing that B is the constraint, we must do something to decide the mix that maximizes profit.

Let's take a look at the five steps of Dr. Goldratt's continuous improvement process. In fact, the first two are enough to find the optimal mix:

IDENTIFY the system's constraint

We know it is resource B.

Decide how to EXPLOIT it

Here you have to use common sense. If resource B prevents us from earning more money, a minute lost there means less money. That means that the time dedicated to P is removed from Q. Then let's see how much money each product generates per minute.

We already know the gross total contribution of each unit of P, $ 45. And of each unit of Q is $ 60.

If for each unit of P 15 minutes are required in B, then each unit of P contributes $ 45/15 min. = $ 3 / min. in the constraint.

Likewise, if for each unit of Q 30 minutes are required, and each unit of Q contributes $ 60 to the total, then each unit of Q contributes $ 2 / min.

With this procedure you reach the same conclusion as with mathematical programming and it is much simpler.

I will summarize it in a table that you can build today in your operation, whatever it is:

Product	Throughput per unit Tu[88]	Minutes of process in the constraint	Tu/minCCR[89]
P	$ 45	15	3
Q	$ 60	30	2

Then, the fourth column indicates the actual profitability of each product. Do it and you will be surprised: some of your favorite

---

[88] Here it is appropriate to put the gross contribution margin, but I assume that you have already read the part where the throughput is defined, so this term will be used.

[89] CCR: Capacity Constrained Resource.

products are not the most profitable, and vice versa.

www.ingramcontent.com/pod-product-compliance
Lightning Source LLC
Chambersburg PA
CBHW020652220526
45464CB00001B/396